Ninja® Foodi®
2-BASKET AIR FRYER
COOKBOOK FOR BEGINNERS

NINJA Foodi

2-BASKET AIR FRYER

COOKBOOK FOR BEGINNERS

80 RECIPES FOR
COMPLETE MEALS USING
DUALZONE TECHNOLOGY

NINJA
TEST
KITCHEN
APPROVED

LAUREN KEATING

PHOTOGRAPHY BY HÉLÈNE DUJARDIN

ROCKRIDGE
PRESS

To Alek, my brother and fellow foodie,
who I can always count on to come up with
off-the-wall recipe ideas.

CONTENTS

INTRODUCTION

AS A FOOD BLOGGER AND COOKBOOK AUTHOR, PEOPLE
often assume that I cook elaborate, gourmet meals every night.
But while I love to cook on the weekends, weeknight cooking is
another story.

I work long hours at my day job and by the time I walk in the door
at night, I'm usually starving and exhausted. My priority is getting
a good meal on the table—fast. I can never seem to resist the call of
the latest great new appliance that promises to help me achieve that
goal. I've found that many of the products that seem the most prom-
ising don't meet my expectations. But I've also come across a few that
really impress me.

Of all the new appliances that have come to market over the past
few years, air fryers are by far my favorite. They're useful for cooking
everything from French fries to roast vegetables, and I love how fast
they are!

However, even though I love air fryers, there's one thing that I
don't love—not being able to cook more than one thing at a time.
The standard air fryer design has just one small basket, so if I wanted
to use the air fryer to cook both a protein and a side dish, I'd have
to make one component and then keep it warm in the oven while
cooking the second. Even though each individual recipe might only
need 10 to 15 minutes to cook, I'm suddenly looking at half an hour to
get dinner on the table.

The Ninja® Foodi® 2-Basket Air Fryer solves this. It has all the
perks of traditional air fryers—easy to use, fast, the ability to cook
super-crispy food with less oil—but it also has two baskets so I can
cook two different foods at the same time.

Its Smart Finish™ and DualZone™ technologies mean that even if two recipes have different temperature or time requirements, they'll be ready at the same time. No more off-loading something to the oven while you wait for your other food to finish cooking. Talk about a game changer!

This book features a collection of my very favorite recipes to make in my Foodi® 2-Basket Air Fryer, all designed to make getting a delicious meal on the table a snap and to take advantage of the DualZone technology for maximum versatility.

Whether you're looking for classic comforts like a Cheeseburger (page 114) or Veggie Burger (page 189) and fries or something more unexpected, like Curry-Crusted Lamb Chops with Baked Brown Sugar Acorn Squash (page 139), you're bound to find a few new favorites in these pages.

Wondering where to start? Here are a few of my personal favorites to get you started: Bacon-Wrapped Dates (page 59), Italian-Style Meatballs with Garlicky Roasted Broccoli (page 108), Beef and Bean Taquitos with Mexican Rice (page 116), Barbecue Chicken Drumsticks with Crispy Kale Chips (page 74), and Baked Mushroom and Mozzarella Frittata with Breakfast Potatoes (page 32). If you have a sweet tooth, you also won't want to miss the Banana Spring Rolls with Hot Fudge Dip (page 196).

I can't wait to hear which recipes are your favorites.
Happy cooking!

1

The Ninja® Foodi® 2-Basket Air Fryer

WHETHER YOU'RE BRAND NEW TO THE NINJA FOODI family or a longtime fan of their innovative kitchen appliances, you're going to be blown away by the new 2-Basket Air Fryer. This convenient device makes getting a delicious meal on the table easier than ever and, if you're anything like me, you'll want to use it every time you walk into the kitchen.

This air fryer can be a little intimidating when you first take it out of the package, but once you get the hang of it, it's so easy to use. In this chapter, I'll cover all the basics to help you get started on the right foot. I'll also go over some frequently asked questions to help set you up with tips for success. Using your air fryer will feel like second nature before you know it.

MEAL PREP IS A SNAP WITH THE NINJA® FOODI® 2-BASKET AIR FRYER

If you've ever cooked with an air fryer, you know how great they are for making fantastically crispy foods quickly. But the Ninja Foodi 2-Basket Air Fryer really takes things to the next level with a brilliant two-basket design that means you can make two things at once! Plus, it's so much more than an air fryer. Additional functions let you bake, broil, reheat, roast, and even dehydrate your favorite foods. It's truly the perfect appliance for busy people looking for quick-and-easy recipes.

Let's dive in and see what makes the Ninja Foodi 2-Basket Air Fryer so great!

Cook Two Things at Once

I can't tell you how many times I've been frustrated because I want to make a side dish that bakes at a totally different temperature than my main course. With this appliance, that's no longer an issue.

The two-basket design means you can make two different recipes at once, whether it's a protein and a side, a dinner and dessert, or two variations of the same food to account for differing tastes or dietary needs.

Since the baskets operate independently of each other, you can set them to two different temperatures or even use different cooking methods. There's also a convenient Smart Finish feature that syncs the baskets so both components of your recipe are done at the same time. That means you don't need to worry about keeping one thing warm while the other finishes cooking.

Crispy Food with Less Oil (or None at All!)

Air fryers are essentially supercharged convection ovens that cook your food by surrounding it with hot air instead of hot oil. This means you can get crispy "fried" foods with just a tablespoon or so of oil—and foods that are naturally higher in fat or sugar often don't require any at all!

Using an air fryer also means you don't need to constantly monitor the temperature of hot oil, reducing the risk of burnt or greasy food.

It Cooks Faster

Since the Foodi® 2-Basket Air Fryer's powerful fan blows hot air directly onto your food as it cooks, it can reduce cook and reheat times by up to 25 percent over conventional cooking methods.

It also doesn't need to preheat the way a traditional oven does, saving valuable time. All you need to do is prep your food and start cooking!

Food Is Juicier

The air fry method sears the outermost layer of food quickly, locking the juices inside. That means your food will come out crispy on the outside and tender on the inside every time. And that isn't just for "fried" food. I love using mine to make succulent roast beef and the juiciest burgers.

It's Versatile

While its ability to air fry two foods at once is the main appeal of the Ninja Foodi 2-Basket Air Fryer, this appliance is so much more than that! Use it to air-broil, air-roast, bake, and even dehydrate your favorite foods and make anything from French fries to beef jerky.

The digital control panel lets you set a wide range of cook times and temperatures manually, so you can make just about anything that you're craving—and have them finish cooking at the same time.

It's Easy to Clean

The nonstick surface helps food slide right off and all its removable parts are nonstick and dishwasher safe. That means you can quickly wash them in between uses. Plus, the appliance's thoughtful design means there aren't any tiny nooks or crannies for food to get stuck in.

MEET YOUR NINJA® FOODI®
2-BASKET AIR FRYER

Congratulations! You're the proud owner of a Ninja Foodi 2-Basket Air Fryer. What now?

Before you start cooking, it's helpful to have a basic understanding of how this appliance works and its basic components. So, let's get acquainted!

Air fryers are small convection ovens that heat from the top and use a powerful fan to blow hot air around food as it cooks. The intense heat dries out the surface of the food, helping it crisp and brown quickly and locking in moisture. When the food is coated with a thin layer of oil before cooking, the result is similar in both taste and texture to deep-fried food, but without the mess or added calories of cooking in hot oil.

When you open the box, you might be surprised to see how simple this machine is. There really isn't much to it, but the components work together to achieve impressive results. Those basic components are:

Air fryer baskets: The two air fryer baskets slide into the base unit, allowing you to make two recipes at the same time. Note that the baskets are not interchangeable, and each will only fit in its designated spot in the main unit. The capacity of each basket depends on what you're making, and whether the food needs to be cooked in a single layer or if it can be stacked. But each one easily holds 2 to 4 servings of most foods. Each basket can fit about 2 pounds of wings or French fries at one time.

Crisper plates: When you remove the baskets from the base unit, you'll see that each one has a perforated crisper plate in the bottom. The crisper plates fit snugly into the baskets but can be lifted out easily. These plates elevate the food, allowing the hot air to circulate around it completely. The crisper plates can also be used to make space for a second layer of food when using the Dehydrate function. Simply place a single layer of food directly in the air fryer basket, then insert the crisper plate and arrange a second layer of food on top. The plates are not needed when using the Roast or Bake functions, but they can be used if desired to allow fat and grease to drain away from your food as it cooks.

There are also some optional accessories that can help maximize the functionality of your 2-Basket Air Fryer. These include:

Broil rack: Some Ninja® Foodi® models also come with a broil rack, which sits inside the basket and lifts food closer to the heating element when using the Broil function. This provides more intense heat and helps the food brown more quickly. If your air fryer didn't come with a broil rack and you want one, they can be purchased on the Ninja website.

Multi-layer rack: The multi-layer rack is similar to the broil rack, but doesn't lift food as high. It allows you to cook two layers of food at once. This is useful if you're feeding a larger family, if you want leftovers, or if you frequently make recipes that need to cook in a single layer and don't want to fuss with making back-to-back batches.

Scale It Up

If you're cooking for a larger family, consider upgrading to the Ninja Foodi XL 2-Basket Air Fryer. This appliance has a larger 10-quart capacity that allows you to roast a small chicken or cook up to 8 pounds of chicken wings at once.

If you're making the recipes from this book in an XL, keep in mind that they may cook slightly faster than the times noted. Be sure to check your food periodically and remove it from the fryer when your desired level of browning has been achieved. You do not need to adjust the temperature.

If you're looking to increase your yield, the recipes in this book can be scaled up by 25 percent if being prepared in an XL. When scaling recipes up, use the original times and temperatures outlined in this book as a guide.

THE CONTROL PANEL

The front of your Ninja® Foodi® 2-Basket Air Fryer features a digital control panel that allows you to select the cook settings for each of the two baskets.

Right in the center of the panel is an LED time display. This display shows your cooking time and temperature as you set them and features a countdown clock so you can easily see how much time remains.

Surrounding the display are several buttons that allow you to set or adjust your cook function, time, and temperature as well as to enable either the Smart Finish™ or Match Cook™ functionality.

It's important to familiarize yourself with what each button does and when to use it.

Cook Functions

After powering on your machine, you'll need to choose from six different cook functions located along the bottom of the control panel. An LED light indicates which function or functions have been selected. This feature really contributes to the versatility of this appliance, since each cook function has its own best uses.

From left to right, the functions are as follows:

Air Broil

Broiling uses intense top-down heat to brown and crisp the top of the food while the convection fan helps circulate the hot air around the basket. This is a great way to add a crispy finish to the top of a casserole, melt toppings, or brown delicate foods without overcooking them. Note that the Air Broil function can only be used in one basket at a time and will not work with Match Cook mode.

Air Fry

If you're looking to mimic the crunchy texture of deep-fried food, this is the function for you! A powerful fan will circulate hot air around your food as it cooks, helping it crisp up while locking moisture inside.

**Ninja Foodi Air Fryer
Unit 6 in 1 Base**

**DualZone Air Fryer
Crisper Plate**

**Ninja Foodi Air Fryer
Left Basket**

**Ninja Foodi Air Fryer
Right Basket**

Roast

This setting defaults to a higher temperature and shorter cook time and is perfect for making tender and juicy roast meats or deliciously caramelized roasted vegetables. Because the small size of the air fryer helps it heat more efficiently than a standard oven, food will roast much more quickly.

Reheat

Gentle heat is great for reheating leftovers and restoring any crispiness that was lost under refrigeration.

Dehydrate

This function delivers steady, low heat that is perfect for dehydrating meats and produce for healthy snacks. You can also use this feature to dry onions, garlic, and herbs to be ground into your own homemade seasoning blends.

Bake

The bake function delivers even heat, making it perfect for decadent treats and desserts with a crisp, caramelized crust.

Operating Buttons

After selecting your cook function, press the button that corresponds to the basket you're cooking in. Then use the temp buttons to the left of the display and the time buttons to the right of the display according to your recipe. Repeat this process with the other basket, if you're using it, then press the Start/Pause button to begin the cooking process.

Zones/baskets

You'll notice two large, numbered buttons to the left and right of the control panel. Press Zone 1 to adjust the settings for the left-hand basket and Zone 2 to adjust the settings for the right-hand basket. These buttons are located on the left and right sides of the control panel, respectively, making it easy to remember which basket each one controls.

Temp arrows

Use the up and down arrows on the left side of the control panel to adjust the cook temperature before or during cooking.

Time arrows

Use the up and down arrows on the right side of the panel to adjust the cook time. This can be used to set the time before cooking begins or to adjust the time as needed during the cooking process. Note that adjusting the cooking time of one basket during the cook cycle will throw off the "smart cook" settings (both Smart Finish and Match Cook), causing the cooking cycle for one basket to stop before the other.

Smart Finish™

If cooking two items that require different cook times, pressing the Smart Finish button will delay the start time of the basket with the shorter cooking time. This ensures both zones finish at the same time, so you don't need to worry about keeping one item warm while the other continues cooking. To use this feature, simply press the Smart Finish button before pressing START.

Match Cook™

This button copies the settings from Zone 1 to Zone 2. This is great if you're making a double batch of the same item and want both baskets to operate with the same cook function, temperature, and time.

Power

The power button, located on the top left of the control panel, turns the unit on and off. When turned off, all cooking functions will stop.

Start/Pause

After selecting your cooking settings, start the cooking process by pressing the Start/Pause button located at the top right of the control panel. To pause cooking without running down the timer, first select the zone you want to pause, then press the Start/Pause button. Press Start/Pause again to resume the cooking process and restart the timer.

Modes

Occasionally, you'll see something on the display screen that you didn't program. Don't worry! This is just to help you know that your air fryer is in either standby mode or that the cooking process has been put on hold.

Standby

When the device is powered on but is not actively cooking, it will enter standby mode if you don't interact with the control panel after 10 minutes. The Power button will be dimly lit and the display screen will go black. Press the Power button to exit standby mode and turn the machine back on.

Hold

When using the Smart Finish™ mode to sync your baskets, one side may start cooking before the other. The display will read HOLD to indicate that cooking for that zone has not started yet.

USING YOUR 2-BASKET AIR FRYER

Now that you've familiarized yourself with the control panel, it's time to explore the intricacies of each cooking function. While they're straightforward, there are some important things to know.

In this section, I'll go over exactly how to use each function, including how to prep the basket and what the maximum allowable time and temperature is.

For Air Fry

When using the Air Fry function, it's important to install the crisper plate in the basket before adding the food. This allows air to circulate and lets moisture drain away so the underside of the food doesn't get soggy. Place your prepared ingredients on the plate, leaving some room between them for the best results and insert the basket into the unit. When using the Air Fry function, the temperature defaults to 390ºF, but can be adjusted from 300ºF to 400ºF. The maximum cooking time is 1 hour, although most foods will require far less time than that.

For Air Broil

When using the Air Broil function, install the crisper plate in the basket to elevate the ingredients. You can also purchase a broil rack that will lift the food closer to the heating element, for even crispier results. When using the Air Broil function, the temperature defaults to the maximum temperature of 450ºF, but can be adjusted as low as 400ºF. The maximum cooking time is 30 minutes. Remember that while you can use a second function in the other basket while broiling, the Air Broil function can only be used in one basket at a time.

For Roast

The crisper plate is not required when using the Roast function, but can be used if desired for easier cleanup or to allow juices to drain away from your food. When using this function, the temperature defaults to 375ºF and can be adjusted between 250ºF and 400ºF. The default cooking time starts at 15 minutes, but can be adjusted up to a maximum cooking time of 4 hours.

For Bake

Place the ingredients directly in the basket and insert the basket in the unit. When baking individual portions such as egg cups, or to keep soft/runny recipes contained like when making dip, it can be helpful to place the ingredients into a ramekin, silicone cupcake liner, or other baking vessel before placing them in the basket. When using the Bake function, the temperature defaults to 325ºF and can be adjusted from 250ºF to 400ºF. The maximum cooking time is 4 hours.

For Reheat

Place the food directly into the basket and insert into the base unit. When a crispier result is desired, such as for reheating pizza, you can use a crisper plate. The temperature can be set from 270ºF to 400ºF and the maximum cook time is 1 hour.

Arrange a single layer of ingredients directly in the basket. Place the crisper plate on top of the ingredients, then top with another layer of ingredients. Adjust the cook temperature between 150ºF and 195ºF and set the timer for up to 12 hours.

To Oil or Not to Oil

While the appeal of air fryers is that they can achieve crispy fried food with far less oil than required for traditional frying, most foods should be spritzed or brushed with a thin layer of oil for the best results.

As the oil heats up, it helps the food brown nicely and also provides an insulating layer to help retain moisture, all contributing to a more traditional flavor and texture for fried foods. Foods that are naturally higher in either fat (like steak) or sugar (like some baked items) will brown well without additional oil.

When using aerosol oil sprays, only spritz the food directly. Do not spritz the components of the air fryer itself, since sprays often contain additives that can build up and damage the nonstick finish.

To prevent burning at high temperatures, be sure to use oil with an appropriate smoke point for the recipe you're making. Neutral-flavored oils that perform well under intense heat up to 450°F include light/refined olive oil (*not* extra-virgin olive oil), vegetable oil, and avocado oil. Note that extra-virgin olive oil should not be used at temperatures over 375°F.

If you prefer to cook without oil, note that your air-fried items will be lighter in color and breading might still appear "raw." Food may also come out dryer if oil isn't added before cooking and individual pieces are more prone to sticking to each other or to the air fryer basket.

COOKING WITH DUALZONE

The Ninja® Foodi® 2-Basket Air Fryer DualZone™ functionality is where this appliance really shines and what makes it so different from traditional air fryers.

This technology controls the temperature and cook time of the two baskets separately. Depending on which function you select, DualZone allows you to either cook two different items for different lengths of time (and also finish simultaneously) or to increase your capacity by making a double batch. Gone are the days of needing to wait until one component of your recipe is done before starting the next.

So, how does it work?

Cooking Two Different Foods

Do you want to make two completely different foods that use two different functions, temperatures, or cook times? Smart Finish automatically delays the start time of one basket, so that both baskets finish at the same time. It's like having a second (faster!) oven.

To use this feature, select the desired cooking function, temperature, and time for each basket, then press the Smart Finish™ button and let the technology take it from there. The zone with the shorter cook time will be delayed and the display will read HOLD until the cook time starts.

You'll really feel like a kitchen ninja when everything is ready at the same time!

Cooking a Double Batch

Match Cook is a great feature if you're cooking the same food in each zone, such as making two flavors of chicken wings.

To use Match Cook™, program Zone 1 as desired, then press the Match Cook button. The settings from Zone 1 will be automatically mirrored by Zone 2. Press Start/Pause to begin cooking.

Note that since the Air Broil function can only be used in one zone at a time, it is not compatible with Match Cook.

If you prefer to start the cooking process at the same time so one basket finishes before the other, simply program both baskets and press Start/Pause without pressing either the Smart Finish™ or Match Cook™ button. This can be useful if the food being cooked in one zone needs to cool or rest before being served.

Shake It Up for Best Results

For the crispiest results, food should be flipped or tossed at least twice during the cooking process. This ensures all sides of the food come into contact with hot air as it circulates around the basket and is especially important when foods are stacked or overlapped and might block air flow.

Press Start/Pause, remove the basket from the unit completely, and give it a good shake to rearrange the food inside. Avoid the urge to remove the basket only partway before shaking it, as this can damage the nonstick finish on the upper edge of the basket. If you prefer, you can also use silicone-tipped tongs to flip the food.

When using Smart Finish, remember to pause both baskets before pulling either of them from the machine to keep them in sync.

To pause just one zone while the other continues cooking, press the button that corresponds to the zone you want to pause, then press the Start/Pause button. To continue the cooking process, simply press the button a second time.

COOKING WITH A SINGLE BASKET

The fact that there are two baskets is one of the biggest attractions of the Ninja® Foodi® 2-Basket Air Fryer, but what if you only want to make a small batch of food? No worries—a single basket can be used just like a traditional air fryer.

To cook with a single basket, place the food in the Zone 1 basket and select your desired cook function. Use the temp and time arrows to program the machine, then press the Start/Pause button to begin cooking.

Keep in mind that since the power doesn't need to be distributed between both baskets, food will cook faster when using only one basket. The recipes in this book were all developed for using both baskets simultaneously, so be sure to check for doneness sooner if you're only making one component. Delicate items will cook in about half the time indicated and heartier items will cook about 20 percent faster when using just one basket.

Adapting Your Favorite Recipes

The Ninja® Foodi® 2-Basket Air Fryer is so versatile that once you've made a few recipes from this book and have gotten the hang of things, you'll naturally want to use it to make all of your old favorites.

Luckily, it's really easy to adapt just about any recipe to be made in your 2-Basket Air Fryer.

The recipes in this cookbook cover a pretty wide range of textures, flavors, and cooking styles, so look for something that's similar to what you want to make and use the cook time and temperature as a guide.

If you can't find a similar recipe, reduce the temperature of your recipe by about 20°F and cut the cook time by about 25 percent. That means a recipe that typically bakes for 30 minutes at 350°F in a traditional oven will bake at 330°F for about 22 minutes when you use your Ninja Foodi. You can use the same 20F°/25-percent rule when using your air fryer to cook frozen foods, like prepared French fries, onion rings, or pizza rolls.

Always keep in mind that foods will cook faster if using a single basket. Additionally, recipes developed for traditional single-basket air fryers might take an extra few minutes if you're using both of the Ninja Foodi's baskets.

FAQS

Because of its two-basket design, the Ninja® Foodi® 2-Basket Air Fryer can be a little different than other appliances you might have used before. There can be a slight learning curve, especially if you're new to air-frying in general.

Below are answers to some of the most frequently asked questions.

Q: Why do some foods blow around when air-frying? How do I solve this?

Because of the air fryer's powerful fan, lightweight foods can sometimes blow around in the basket. This generally isn't a problem, but it can be annoying if you're making a sandwich or other layered food that won't stay together. To help prevent this, use a toothpick or skewer to secure foods in place.

Q: When should I use the crisper plate?

The crisper plates should be used when you want food to come out crispy, typically when using the Air Fry or Air Broil functions. The plate raises the food from the bottom of the basket so air can flow around it freely and to allow juices and grease to drain away.

Q: Why didn't my food cook fully?

Make sure the basket is inserted completely into the machine. To ensure food cooks evenly when air-frying, make sure ingredients are arranged in a single layer without overlapping (unless the recipe indicates that foods can be stacked) and turn or toss the food at least twice during the cooking process.

The extra power needed required by the two-basket design also means cooking times are often slightly longer than called for in recipes developed for traditional single-basket air fryers. Overfilling the machine can also necessitate longer cook times.

Variables like moisture content and size can also affect the cooking time, so start checking for doneness a little before the timer goes off and don't be afraid to add more time if you think it's necessary.

Q: Why did my food burn?

For best results, start checking for doneness about three-quarters of the way through the cooking process and remove food when the desired level of brownness and a safe internal temperature has been achieved. I highly recommend investing in an instant-read thermometer, since food may appear done before the center has fully cooked.

Keep in mind that food will cook faster if using a single basket or if the appliance is still warm from cooking back-to-back batches. A second batch of the same recipe might cook in half the time.

To avoid overcooking, remove food from the basket immediately after the cook time is complete.

Q: Can I air fry ingredients with batter?

Yes! When using wet batters, make sure the batter is thick enough to stay on the food without sliding off and line the crisper plate with parchment paper or aluminum foil to prevent the batter from dripping through the perforations.

For breaded items, it's important to use the proper breading technique. It should be done in this order: 1) dust the food with flour, 2) dip into beaten egg, and 3) coat with bread crumbs. Press the bread crumbs into the food to help them stick and prevent the air fryer's fan from blowing them off.

Q: Do I need to preheat the air fryer?

No, the Ninja® Foodi® 2-Basket Air Fryer does not need to be preheated before adding your ingredients. All recipes in this book are written to begin with the appliance nonheated.

Q: Can I use aluminum foil in the air fryer?

Yes, the use of aluminum foil is totally okay and some recipes recommend it.

Q: **Is an air fryer the same as a convection oven?**

Air fryers and convection ovens are similar in that they use a fan to circulate hot air around food as it cooks, but the smaller size and more powerful fan of an air fryer gets food crispier and cooks it faster.

Q: **Why does my air fryer smell funny?**

New air fryers are coated with a food-safe protective coating that can sometimes emit a slight plastic-y smell when heated. It will not impact the taste of your food and will go away after the first few uses. If your air fryer smells like smoke, power it down and unplug it. Let it cool, then clean it thoroughly. Crumbs or food residue can bake onto the air fryer and burn.

Top Tips for 2-Basket Air Fryer Success

Here are my top tips to help you get the most from your Ninja Foodi 2-Basket Air Fryer.

1. **Don't overcrowd the baskets.** If you add too much food, it won't cook evenly and could end up sticking to the basket. For consistent browning, make sure ingredients are arranged in an even layer on the bottom of the basket with no overlapping.

2. **Give your food a light mist of oil before air-frying it.** This will add flavor and help the food crisp up.

3. **Shake or turn your foods.** Do this at least twice during the cooking process to ensure food cooks evenly.

4. **Always pause the timer to stop the clock on both baskets by pressing Start/Pause.** This is important even if removing just one basket from the base unit, especially when using the Smart Finish feature.

5. **Clean the air fryer after each use.** All of its removable parts are dishwasher safe, so it's easy to keep it clean.

6. **Start checking food for doneness 5 minutes before the scheduled cook time is complete.** Cooking times will vary based on a variety of factors, including the size of individual items. Stop cooking as soon as the desired level of crispiness has been achieved and a safe internal temperature has been reached.

7. **Invest in an instant-read digital thermometer.** Hand in hand with tip 6 above, a digital thermometer can easily tell you if food has reached a safe temperature.

8. **Secure light foods with wooden toothpicks or skewers to prevent the fan from blowing them around.**

9. **Soak raw potatoes in cold water for 15 to 20 minutes** before air-frying to remove excess starch, then coat with at least 1 tablespoon of oil for the crispiest results.

10. **Remove food from the baskets immediately** after the cook time is complete to avoid overcooking.

KEEPING IT CLEAN

To keep your air fryer in tip-top condition, it's important to keep it clean. This is the easiest to do immediately after use, before food residue and grease have time to solidify and stick to the crisper plates or baskets. If you're making something especially messy or gooey, lining the air fryer basket with parchment paper can also help make cleanup easier.

The removable parts of the air fryer are dishwasher safe, but washing them by hand can help protect the finish and increase its longevity. The nonstick surface of the drawers and crisper plates makes them super easy to wash by hand, since crumbs and grease slide right off.

If food is stuck on the crisper plates or baskets, let them soak in a sink filled with warm, soapy water until it has softened. Do not force food off or use abrasive cleaners, which can damage the nonstick finish. If necessary, you can clean them with a soft brush.

To clean the base of the air fryer, unplug it and wipe it clean with a damp cloth. The base unit contains electrical components, so it's important to *never* submerge it in water or attempt to clean it in a dishwasher.

ABOUT THE RECIPES

Now that we've covered the basics, let's get cooking!

This book contains some of my very favorite recipes, all adapted to make the most of the Ninja® Foodi® 2-Basket Air Fryer's ability to cook two things at once.

For main dishes, each recipe was developed to serve as a complete meal with a protein and a complementary side dish. For appetizers and desserts, the recipes either have two complementary components or the baskets are used to make a double batch of one recipe with two variations that could be served together to account for different tastes (like the Buffalo Wings and sweeter Honey-Garlic Wings on page 56). The recipes also use the air fryer's Smart Finish and

Match Cook™ technologies to ensure all components of the meal are ready at the same time.

Since each recipe can also stand alone, it's like you're really getting 160 recipes in this book! To that end, I took care to write each recipe so that you can easily follow the directions for a single component, making it easier to mix and match to your heart's content. Throughout the book, I've also made notes about some of my favorite swaps. Be sure to check out the Mix and Match Recipe Cooking Chart (page 226) for an easy resource to help with your menu planning.

Because I always strive to make my recipes accessible to people with a variety of lifestyles and nutritional needs, and since so many people are attracted to air fryers for their nutritional benefits and ability to cook with less oil, each recipe includes both nutritional information and convenient labels that address the following dietary concerns:

- Dairy-Free

- Gluten-Free

- Nut-Free

- Vegan or Vegetarian

I have also included helpful tips throughout to help you achieve maximum success and make the most out of your air fryer. Keep your eyes peeled for the following:

Prep tip: These are tips and hacks that help make preparing the recipe easier or faster.

Variation: Easy additions or swaps that change the flavor profile of the recipe for maximum versatility.

Super swap: A handy reference of other recipes that pair well with each main course, for the ultimate flexibility.

Spinach and Red Pepper Egg Cups with Coffee-Glazed Canadian Bacon, *page 28*

2

Breakfast

Buttermilk Biscuits with Roasted Stone Fruit Compote

SERVES 4

These oh-so-tasty biscuits are a real treat on a weekend morning. They're tall and flaky and are a heavenly breakfast experience when served warm and topped with butter and a jammy roasted fruit compote. To get the best rise on your biscuits, press a biscuit cutter or round cookie cutter straight into the dough, then lift it back out without twisting.

NUT-FREE, VEGETARIAN

Prep time: 15 minutes
Cook time: 20 minutes

FOR THE BISCUITS

1⅓ cups all-purpose flour

2 teaspoons sugar

2 teaspoons baking powder

½ teaspoon baking soda

½ teaspoon kosher salt

4 tablespoons (½ stick) very cold unsalted butter

½ cup plus 1 tablespoon low-fat buttermilk

FOR THE FRUIT COMPOTE

2 peaches, peeled and diced

2 plums, peeled and diced

¼ cup water

2 teaspoons honey

⅛ teaspoon ground ginger (optional)

1. To prep the biscuits: In a small bowl, combine the flour, sugar, baking powder, baking soda, and salt. Using the large holes on a box grater, grate in the butter. Stir in the buttermilk to form a thick dough.

2. Place the dough on a lightly floured surface and gently pat it into a ½-inch-thick disc. Fold the dough in half, then rotate the whole thing 90 degrees, pat into a ½-inch thick disc and fold again. Repeat until you have folded the dough four times.

3. Pat the dough out a final time into a ½-inch-thick disc and use a 3-inch biscuit cutter to cut 4 biscuits from the dough (discard the scraps).

4. To prep the fruit compote: In a large bowl, stir together the peaches, plums, water, honey, and ginger (if using).

5. To cook the biscuits and compote: Install a crisper plate in the Zone 1 basket, place the biscuits in the basket, and insert the basket in the unit. Place the fruit in the Zone 2 basket and insert the basket in the unit.

6. Select Zone 1, select AIR FRY, set the temperature to 400°F, and set the time to 10 minutes.

7. Select Zone 2, select ROAST, set the temperature to 350°F, and set the time to 20 minutes. Select SMART FINISH.™

8. Press START/PAUSE to begin cooking.

9. When the Zone 2 timer reads 10 minutes, press START/PAUSE. Remove the basket and stir the compote. Reinsert the basket and press START/PAUSE to resume cooking.

10. When cooking is complete, the biscuits will be golden brown and crisp on top and the fruit will be soft. Transfer the biscuits to a plate to cool. Lightly mash the fruit to form a thick, jammy sauce.

11. Split the biscuits in half horizontally and serve topped with fruit compote.

Per serving: Calories: 332; Total fat: 12g; Saturated fat: 7.5g; Carbohydrates: 50g; Fiber: 2.5g; Protein: 6g; Sodium: 350mg

Prep tip: If you don't have a biscuit cutter, you can use this dough to make drop biscuits. Use a ¼-cup measure to divide the dough into portions and drop directly into the basket. Drop biscuits won't have the same flaky layers as biscuits that are rolled and cut, but they taste just as good!

Lemon-Cream Cheese Danishes // Cherry Danishes

SERVES 4

These Danishes are every bit as delicious as the ones from your favorite bakery, but they're so easy to make at home with store-bought puff pastry! Cheese Danishes are my absolute favorite breakfast, and I love how the sweetened cream cheese complements the tangy lemon curd filling in the lemon-cream cheese Danishes. If you're looking for a dairy-free option, give the cherry version a try.

VEGETARIAN

Prep time: 10 minutes
Cook time: 15 minutes

FOR THE CREAM CHEESE DANISHES

1 ounce (2 tablespoons) cream cheese, at room temperature

1 teaspoon granulated sugar

¼ teaspoon freshly squeezed lemon juice

⅛ teaspoon vanilla extract

½ sheet frozen puff pastry, thawed

2 tablespoons lemon curd

1 large egg yolk

1 tablespoon water

FOR THE CHERRY DANISHES

½ sheet frozen puff pastry, thawed

2 tablespoons cherry preserves

1 teaspoon coarse sanding sugar

1. To prep the cream cheese Danishes: In a small bowl, mix the cream cheese, granulated sugar, lemon juice, and vanilla.

2. Cut the puff pastry sheet into 2 squares. Cut a ½-inch-wide strip from each side of the pastry. Brush the edges of the pastry square with water, then layer the strips along the edges, pressing gently to adhere and form a border around the outside of the pastry.

3. Divide the cream cheese mixture between the two pastries, then top each with 1 tablespoon of lemon curd.

4. In a second small bowl, whisk together the egg yolk and water (this will be used for the cherry Danishes, too). Brush the exposed edges of the pastry with half the egg wash.

5. To prep the cherry Danishes: Cut the puff pastry sheet into 2 squares. Cut a ½-inch-wide strip from each side of the pastry. Brush the edges of the pastry square with water, then layer the strips along the edges, pressing gently to adhere and form a border around the outside of the pastry.

6. Spoon 1 tablespoon of cherry preserves into the center of each pastry.

7. Brush the exposed edges of the pastry with the remaining egg wash, then sprinkle with the sanding sugar.

8. To cook both Danishes: Install a crisper plate in each of the two baskets. Place the cream cheese Danishes in the Zone 1 basket and insert the basket in the unit. Place the cherry Danishes in the Zone 2 basket and insert the basket in the unit.

9. Select Zone 1, select AIR FRY, set the temperature to 330°F, and set the time to 15 minutes. Select MATCH COOK™ to match Zone 2 settings to Zone 1.

10. Press START/PAUSE to begin cooking.

11. When cooking is complete, transfer the Danishes to a wire rack to cool. Serve warm.

Variation: Use your favorite fruit preserves or canned pie filling in place of the lemon curd and cherry preserves. Some of my favorites include seedless raspberry preserves and blueberry pie filling.

Per serving (1 lemon-cream cheese Danish): *Calories: 415; Total fat: 24g; Saturated fat: 12g; Carbohydrates: 51g; Fiber: 1.5g; Protein: 7g; Sodium: 274mg*

Per serving (1 cherry Danish): *Calories: 315; Total fat: 16g; Saturated fat: 8g; Carbohydrates: 45g; Fiber: 1.5g; Protein: 5g; Sodium: 215mg*

Spinach and Red Pepper Egg Cups with Coffee-Glazed Canadian Bacon

SERVES 6

Egg cups are a great way to enjoy a healthy breakfast on the go. These individual servings of scrambled eggs are sturdy enough to be eaten like a muffin, but still have a delicious creamy texture. Here, I've paired them with tasty Canadian bacon coated in a glaze that's inspired by red-eye gravy.

GLUTEN-FREE, NUT-FREE

Prep time: 10 minutes
Cook time: 13 minutes

FOR THE EGG CUPS

4 large eggs

¼ cup heavy (whipping) cream

¼ teaspoon kosher salt

¼ teaspoon freshly ground black pepper

½ cup roasted red peppers (about 1 whole pepper), drained and chopped

½ cup baby spinach, chopped

FOR THE CANADIAN BACON

¼ cup brewed coffee

2 tablespoons maple syrup

1 tablespoon light brown sugar

6 slices Canadian bacon

1. **To prep the egg cups:** In a medium bowl, whisk together the eggs and cream until well combined with a uniform, light color. Stir in the salt, black pepper, roasted red peppers, and spinach until combined.

2. Divide the egg mixture among 6 silicone muffin cups.

3. **To prep the Canadian bacon:** In a small bowl, whisk together the coffee, maple syrup, and brown sugar.

4. Using a basting brush, brush the glaze onto both sides of each slice of bacon.

5. To cook the egg cups and Canadian bacon: Install a crisper plate in each of the two baskets. Place the egg cups in the Zone 1 basket and insert the basket in the unit. Place the glazed bacon in the Zone 2 basket, making sure the slices don't overlap, and insert the basket in the unit. It is okay if the bacon overlaps a little bit.

6. Select Zone 1, select BAKE, set the temperature to 325ºF, and set the time to 13 minutes.

7. Select Zone 2, select AIR FRY, set the temperature to 400ºF, and set the time to 5 minutes. Select SMART FINISH.™

8. Press START/PAUSE to begin cooking.

9. When the Zone 2 timer reads 2 minutes, press START/PAUSE. Remove the basket and use silicone-tipped tongs to flip the bacon. Reinsert the basket and press START/PAUSE to resume cooking.

10. When cooking is complete, serve the egg cups with the Canadian bacon.

Per serving: *Calories: 180; Total fat: 9.5g; Saturated fat: 4.5g; Carbohydrates: 9g; Fiber: 0g; Protein: 14g; Sodium: 688mg*

Variation: Instead of Canadian bacon, you can also make this recipe with a ham steak. Increase the cooking time in the Zone 2 basket to 10 minutes.

Blueberry Coffee Cake and Maple Sausage Patties

SERVES 6

This blueberry coffee cake was inspired by a recent trip to Maine, where blueberries seemed to be in everything. You can use fresh blueberries or frozen berries straight from your freezer. I love the way this simple coffee cake pairs with sweet and savory maple breakfast sausage, and I hope you will, too.

NUT-FREE

Prep time: 20 minutes, plus 5 minutes to cool
Cook time: 25 minutes

FOR THE COFFEE CAKE

- 6 tablespoons unsalted butter, at room temperature, divided
- ⅓ cup granulated sugar
- 1 large egg
- 1 teaspoon vanilla extract
- ¼ cup whole milk
- 1½ cups all-purpose flour, divided
- 1 teaspoon baking powder
- ¼ teaspoon salt
- 1 cup blueberries
- ¼ cup packed light brown sugar
- ½ teaspoon ground cinnamon

FOR THE SAUSAGE PATTIES

- ½ pound ground pork
- 2 tablespoons maple syrup
- ½ teaspoon dried sage
- ½ teaspoon dried thyme
- 1½ teaspoons kosher salt
- ½ teaspoon crushed fennel seeds
- ½ teaspoon red pepper flakes (optional)
- ¼ teaspoon freshly ground black pepper

1. **To prep the coffee cake:** In a large bowl, cream together 4 tablespoons of butter with the granulated sugar. Beat in the egg, vanilla, and milk.

2. Stir in 1 cup of flour, along with the baking soda and salt, to form a thick batter. Fold in the blueberries.

3. In a second bowl, mix the remaining 2 tablespoons of butter, remaining ½ cup of flour, the brown sugar, and cinnamon to form a dry crumbly mixture.

4. To prep the sausage patties: In a large bowl, mix the pork, maple syrup, sage, thyme, salt, fennel seeds, red pepper flakes (if using), and black pepper until just combined.

5. Divide the mixture into 6 equal patties about ½ inch thick.

6. To cook the coffee cake and sausage patties: Spread the cake batter into the Zone 1 basket, top with the crumble mixture, and insert the basket in the unit. Install a crisper plate in the Zone 2 basket, add the sausage patties in a single layer, and insert the basket in the unit.

7. Select Zone 1, select BAKE, set the temperature to 350°F, and set the time to 25 minutes.

8. Select Zone 2, select AIR FRY, set the temperature to 375°F, and set the time to 12 minutes. Select SMART FINISH.™

9. Press START/PAUSE to begin cooking.

10. When the Zone 2 timer reads 6 minutes, press START/PAUSE. Remove the basket and use silicone-tipped tongs to flip the sausage patties. Reinsert the basket and press START/PAUSE to resume cooking.

11. When cooking is complete, let the coffee cake cool for at least 5 minutes, then cut into 6 slices. Serve warm or at room temperature with the sausage patties.

Per serving: Calories: 395; Total fat: 15g; Saturated fat: 8g; Carbohydrates: 53g; Fiber: 1.5g; Protein: 14g; Sodium: 187mg

Prep tip: You can use fresh or frozen berries for this recipe. If using frozen berries, do not thaw them before adding them to the batter.

Baked Mushroom and Mozzarella Frittata with Breakfast Potatoes

SERVES 4

Frittatas are a welcome addition to any brunch. This version, studded with mushrooms and gooey mozzarella cheese, is inspired by one of my favorite brunch spots. I'll be honest though: I think I like my version even better than theirs! The eggs come out super soft and fluffy, with a texture that far surpasses a traditional frittata. Round out your meal by serving this baked egg dish with crispy breakfast potatoes.

GLUTEN-FREE, NUT-FREE, VEGETARIAN

Prep time: 10 minutes
Cook time: 35 minutes

FOR THE FRITTATA

8 large eggs

⅓ cup whole milk

1 teaspoon kosher salt

½ teaspoon freshly ground black pepper

1 cup sliced cremini mushrooms (about 2 ounces)

1 teaspoon olive oil

2 ounces part-skim mozzarella cheese, cut into ½-inch cubes

FOR THE POTATOES

2 russet potatoes, cut into ½-inch cubes

1 tablespoon olive oil

½ teaspoon garlic powder

¼ teaspoon kosher salt

¼ teaspoon freshly ground black pepper

1. **To prep the frittata:** In a large bowl, whisk together the eggs, milk, salt, and pepper. Stir in the mushrooms.

2. **To prep the potatoes:** In a large bowl, combine the potatoes, olive oil, garlic powder, salt, and black pepper.

3. **To cook the frittata and potatoes:** Brush the bottom of the Zone 1 basket with 1 teaspoon of olive oil. Add the egg mixture to the basket, top with the mozzarella cubes, and insert the basket in the unit. Install a crisper plate in the Zone 2 basket. Place the potatoes in the basket and insert the basket in the unit.

4. Select Zone 1, select BAKE, set the temperature to 350ºF, and set the time to 30 minutes.

5. Select Zone 2, select AIR FRY, set the temperature to 400ºF, and set the time to 35 minutes. Select SMART FINISH.™

6. Press START/PAUSE to begin cooking.

7. When the Zone 2 timer reads 15 minutes, press START/PAUSE. Remove the basket and shake the potatoes for 10 seconds. Reinsert the basket and press START/PAUSE to resume cooking.

8. When cooking is complete, the frittata will pull away from the edges of the basket and the potatoes will be golden brown. Transfer the frittata to a cutting board and cut into 4 portions. Serve with the potatoes.

Per serving: *Calories: 307; Total fat: 17g; Saturated fat: 5.5g; Carbohydrates: 18g; Fiber: 1g; Protein: 19g; Sodium: 600mg*

Sausage Hash and Baked Eggs

SERVES 4

This hearty breakfast is perfect for a lazy weekend morning. The sausage and potatoes are perfectly tender-crisp from the air fryer, and it's so good topped with the creamy eggs. This recipe will produce medium yolks; if you prefer your yolks harder, add an extra minute to the cook time.

DAIRY-FREE, GLUTEN-FREE, NUT-FREE

Prep time: 10 minutes
Cook time: 30 minutes

FOR THE HASH

2 yellow potatoes (about 1 pound), cut into ½-inch pieces

4 garlic cloves, minced

1 teaspoon kosher salt

¼ teaspoon freshly ground black pepper

2 tablespoons olive oil

½ pound pork breakfast sausage meat

1 small yellow onion, diced

1 red bell pepper, diced

1 teaspoon Italian seasoning

FOR THE EGGS

Nonstick cooking spray

4 large eggs

4 tablespoons water

1. **To prep the hash:** In a large bowl, combine the potatoes, garlic, salt, black pepper, and olive oil and toss to coat. Crumble in the sausage and mix until combined.

2. **To prep the eggs:** Mist 4 silicone muffin cups with cooking spray. Crack 1 egg into each muffin cup. Top each egg with 1 tablespoon of water.

3. **To cook the hash and eggs:** Install a crisper plate in the Zone 1 basket. Place the sausage and potato mixture in the Zone 1 basket and insert the basket in the unit. Place the egg cups in the Zone 2 basket and insert the basket in the unit.

4. Select Zone 1, select AIR FRY, set the temperature to 400°F, and set the time to 30 minutes.

5. Select Zone 2, select BAKE, set the temperature to 325°F, and set the time to 12 minutes. Select SMART FINISH.™

6. Press START/PAUSE to begin cooking.

7. When the Zone 1 timer reads 20 minutes, press START/PAUSE. Remove the basket and add the onion, bell pepper, and Italian seasoning to the hash. Mix until combined, breaking up any large pieces of sausage. Reinsert the basket and press START/PAUSE to resume cooking.

8. When cooking is complete, serve the hash topped with an egg.

Per serving: *Calories: 400; Total fat: 23g; Saturated fat: 5.5g; Carbohydrates: 31g; Fiber: 2g; Protein: 19g; Sodium: 750mg*

Variation: If you prefer, you can use crumbled turkey sausage or vegetarian sausage in place of the breakfast sausage.

Strawberry Baked Oats // Chocolate Peanut Butter Baked Oats

SERVES 12

These two oatmeal recipes bring me straight back to my childhood, when I made microwavable packets of oatmeal for breakfast almost every morning. But instead of being a thick porridge, this baked oatmeal has a firm texture that's like a cross between oatmeal and a soft granola bar. Whether you have a sweet tooth or not, you'll love these recipes!

GLUTEN-FREE, VEGETARIAN

Prep time: 10 minutes
Cook time: 15 minutes

FOR THE STRAWBERRY OATS

1 cup whole milk

1 cup heavy (whipping) cream

½ cup maple syrup

2 teaspoons vanilla extract

2 large eggs

2 cups old-fashioned oats

2 teaspoons baking powder

½ teaspoon ground cinnamon

¼ teaspoon kosher salt

1½ cups diced strawberries

FOR THE CHOCOLATE PEANUT BUTTER OATS

2 very ripe bananas

½ cup maple syrup

¼ cup unsweetened cocoa powder

2 teaspoons vanilla extract

2 teaspoons baking powder

2 large eggs

½ teaspoon kosher salt

2 cups old-fashioned oats

2 tablespoons peanut butter

1. **To prep the strawberry oats:** In a large bowl, combine the milk, cream, maple syrup, vanilla, and eggs. Stir in the oats, baking powder, cinnamon, and salt until fully combined. Fold in the strawberries.

2. **To prep the chocolate peanut butter oats:** In a large bowl, mash the banana with a fork. Stir in the maple syrup, cocoa powder, vanilla, baking powder, and salt until smooth. Beat in the eggs. Stir in the oats until everything is combined.

3. To bake the oats: Place the strawberry oatmeal in the Zone 1 basket and insert the basket in the unit. Place the chocolate peanut butter oatmeal in the Zone 2 basket. Add ½ teaspoon dollops of peanut butter on top and insert the basket in the unit.

4. Select Zone 1, select BAKE, set the temperature to 320ºF, and set the time to 15 minutes. Select MATCH COOK™ to match Zone 2 settings to Zone 1.

5. Press START/PAUSE to begin cooking.

6. When cooking is complete, serve each oatmeal in a shallow bowl.

Per serving (strawberry): *Calories: 367; Total fat: 19g; Saturated fat: 11g; Carbohydrates: 42g; Fiber: 3.5g; Protein: 8g; Sodium: 102mg*

Per serving (chocolate peanut butter): *Calories: 270; Total fat: 7g; Saturated fat: 2g; Carbohydrates: 48g; Fiber: 5g; Protein: 8g; Sodium: 51mg*

Variation: For a fluffy, cake-like version of either of the baked oats, puree the ingredients in a blender or food processor before pouring into the air fryer basket. If making the strawberry version, hold back the diced fresh strawberries and stir them in after you have pureed the rest of the ingredients.

Pumpkin French Toast Casserole with Sweet and Spicy Twisted Bacon

SERVES 4

This sweet and salty breakfast has an extra special twist—literally! Twisting bacon before cooking results in crispy edges and a delightfully chewy center. It also makes the bacon slices a little shorter, so they fit perfectly in an air fryer basket. I love adding a pinch of cayenne pepper to help balance out the sweetness of the custardy French toast casserole.

DAIRY-FREE, NUT-FREE

Prep time: 10 minutes, plus 10 minutes to soak and 3 minutes to cool
Cook time: 35 minutes

FOR THE FRENCH TOAST CASSEROLE

3 large eggs

1 cup unsweetened almond milk

1 cup canned unsweetened pumpkin puree

2 teaspoons pumpkin pie spice

¼ cup packed light brown sugar

1 teaspoon vanilla extract

6 cups French bread cubes

1 teaspoon vegetable oil

¼ cup maple syrup

FOR THE BACON

2 tablespoons light brown sugar

⅛ teaspoon cayenne pepper

8 slices bacon

1. **To prep the French toast casserole:** In a shallow bowl, whisk together the eggs, almond milk, pumpkin puree, pumpkin pie spice, brown sugar, and vanilla.

2. Add the bread cubes to the egg mixture, making sure the bread is fully coated in the custard. Let sit for at least 10 minutes to allow the bread to soak up the custard.

3. **To prep the bacon:** In a small bowl, combine the brown sugar and cayenne.

CONTINUED >

Pumpkin French Toast Casserole with Sweet and Spicy Twisted Bacon continued

Prep tip: The French toast casserole can be prepared up to 2 days in advance. If prepping it ahead, cover the bread and custard mixture with plastic wrap and refrigerate. Add 5 minutes to the cook time.

4. Arrange the bacon on a cutting board in a single layer. Evenly sprinkle the strips with the brown sugar mixture. Fold the bacon strip in half lengthwise. Hold one end of the bacon steady and twist the other end so the bacon resembles a straw.

5. **To cook the casserole and bacon:** Brush the Zone 1 basket with the oil. Pour the French toast casserole into the Zone 1 basket, drizzle with maple syrup, and insert the basket in the unit. Install a crisper plate in the Zone 2 basket, add the bacon twists in a single layer, and insert the basket in the unit. For the best fit, arrange the bacon twists across the unit, front to back.

6. Select Zone 1, select BAKE, set the temperature to 330°F, and set the time to 35 minutes.

7. Select Zone 2, select AIR FRY, set the temperature to 400°F, and set the time to 12 minutes. Select SMART FINISH.™

8. Press START/PAUSE to begin cooking.

9. When cooking is complete, transfer the bacon to a plate lined with paper towels. Let cool for 2 to 3 minutes before serving with the French toast casserole.

Per serving: Calories: 601; Total fat: 28g; Saturated fat: 9g; Carbohydrates: 67g; Fiber: 2.5g; Protein: 17g; Sodium: 814mg

Cinnamon-Raisin Bagels //
Everything Bagels

SERVES 4

When it comes to breakfast, bagels are a New York City staple. The air fryer turns out some of my favorites! They're crispy on the outside and perfectly chewy on the inside. The two-basket design of the Ninja® Foodi® means you can keep two flavors of bagels separate while they cook—no more worrying about garlic or onion flakes creeping onto your sweet cinnamon-raisin bagels.

NUT-FREE, VEGETARIAN

Prep time: 15 minutes, plus 5 minutes to cool
Cook time: 14 minutes

FOR THE BAGEL DOUGH
1 cup all-purpose flour, plus more for dusting
2 teaspoons baking powder
1 teaspoon kosher salt
1 cup reduced-fat plain Greek yogurt

FOR THE CINNAMON-RAISIN BAGELS
¼ cup raisins
½ teaspoon ground cinnamon

FOR THE EVERYTHING BAGELS
¼ teaspoon poppy seeds
¼ teaspoon sesame seeds
¼ teaspoon dried minced garlic
¼ teaspoon dried minced onion

FOR THE EGG WASH
1 large egg
1 tablespoon water

1. **To prep the bagels:** In a large bowl, combine the flour, baking powder, and salt. Stir in the yogurt to form a soft dough. Turn the dough out onto a lightly floured surface and knead five to six times, until it is smooth and elastic. Divide the dough in half.

2. Knead the raisins and cinnamon into one dough half. Leave the other dough half plain.

CONTINUED >

Prep tip: You can use 1 teaspoon of store-bought everything bagel seasoning instead of making your own.

Variation: Swap the raisins for dried cranberries and the cinnamon for 1 teaspoon of grated orange zest to make delicious cranberry-orange bagels.

3. Divide both portions of dough in half to form a total of 4 balls of dough (2 cinnamon-raisin and 2 plain). Roll each ball of dough into a rope about 8 inches long. Shape each rope into a ring and pinch the ends to seal.

4. To prep the everything bagels: In a small bowl, mix together the poppy seeds, sesame seeds, garlic, and onion.

5. To prep the egg wash: In a second small bowl, beat together the egg and water. Brush the egg wash on top of each bagel.

6. Generously sprinkle the everything seasoning over the top of the 2 plain bagels.

7. To cook the bagels: Install a crisper plate in each of the two baskets. Place the cinnamon-raisin bagels in the Zone 1 basket and insert the basket in the unit. For best results, the bagels should not overlap in the basket. Place the everything bagels in the Zone 2 basket and insert the basket in the unit.

8. Select Zone 1, select AIR FRY, set the temperature to 325°F, and set the time to 14 minutes. Select MATCH COOK™ to match Zone 2 settings to Zone 1.

9. Press START/PAUSE to begin cooking.

10. When cooking is complete, use silicone-tipped tongs to transfer the bagels to a cutting board. Let cool for 2 to 3 minutes before cutting and serving.

Per serving (1 cinnamon-raisin bagel): *Calories: 238; Total fat: 3g; Saturated fat: 1g; Carbohydrates: 43g; Fiber: 1.5g; Protein: 11g; Sodium: 321mg*

Per serving (1 everything bagel): *Calories: 181; Total fat: 3g; Saturated fat: 1g; Carbohydrates: 27g; Fiber: 1g; Protein: 11g; Sodium: 319mg*

Glazed Apple Fritters //
Glazed Peach Fritters

SERVES 4

These delicious fritters are the perfect way to use up extra fruit. And the cinnamon glaze is the ideal finishing touch! Apple fritters are a classic fall treat, but I also love making these fritters with fresh summer peaches. For the best results, choose firm fruit that will hold its shape as it's cooked.

NUT-FREE, VEGETARIAN

Prep time: 15 minutes
Cook time: 12 minutes

FOR THE FRITTERS
¾ cup all-purpose flour

2 tablespoons granulated sugar

1 teaspoon baking powder

½ teaspoon kosher salt

½ teaspoon ground cinnamon

⅓ cup whole milk

2 tablespoons cold unsalted butter, grated

1 large egg

1 teaspoon fresh lemon juice

1 apple, peeled and diced

1 peach, peeled and diced

FOR THE GLAZE
½ cup powdered sugar

1 tablespoon whole milk

½ teaspoon vanilla extract

½ teaspoon ground cinnamon

Pinch salt

1. **To prep the fritters:** In a large bowl, combine the flour, granulated sugar, baking powder, salt, and cinnamon. Stir in the milk, butter, egg, and lemon juice to form a thick batter.

2. Transfer half of the batter to a second bowl. Fold the apples into one bowl and the peaches into the other.

3. **To prep the glaze:** In a small bowl, whisk together the powdered sugar, milk, vanilla, cinnamon, and salt until smooth. Set aside.

4. To cook the fritters: Install a crisper plate in each of the two baskets. Drop two ¼-cup scoops of the apple fritter batter into the Zone 1 basket and insert the basket in the unit. Drop two ¼-cup scoops of the peach fritter batter into the Zone 2 basket and insert the basket in the unit.

5. Select Zone 1, select AIR FRY, set the temperature to 345ºF, and set the time to 10 minutes.

6. Select Zone 2, select AIR FRY, set the temperature to 345ºF, and set the time to 12 minutes. Select SMART FINISH.™

7. Press START/PAUSE to begin cooking.

8. When cooking is complete, transfer the fritters to a wire rack and drizzle the glaze over them. Serve warm or at room temperature.

Per serving (1 apple fritter): *Calories: 298; Total fat: 8g; Saturated fat: 4.5g; Carbohydrates: 53g; Fiber: 3g; Protein: 5g; Sodium: 170mg*

Per serving (1 peach fritter): *Calories: 280; Total fat: 8g; Saturated fat: 4.5g; Carbohydrates: 47g; Fiber: 1.5g; Protein: 5g; Sodium: 169mg*

Roasted Tomato Bruschetta with Toasty Garlic Bread, *page 54*

3

Appetizers and Snacks

Miso-Glazed Shishito Peppers // Charred Lemon Shishito Peppers

SERVES 4

Trendy shishito peppers have been easy to find in major grocery stores lately, and I couldn't be happier about it. These little peppers are mild and slightly sweet, with a nice smoky flavor from the charring. Occasionally, you'll get one that's unexpectedly spicy, so keep that in mind! These make a great appetizer on their own or dipped in garlic aioli. Although miso is usually made only with soybeans, some versions use barley, so be sure to read the label if you need this to be gluten-free.

NUT-FREE, DAIRY-FREE, GLUTEN-FREE, VEGAN

Prep time: 5 minutes
Cook time: 10 minutes

FOR THE MISO-GLAZED PEPPERS

2 tablespoons vegetable oil

2 tablespoons water

1 tablespoon white miso

1 teaspoon grated fresh ginger

½ pound shishito peppers

FOR THE CHARRED LEMON PEPPERS

½ pound shishito peppers

1 lemon, cut into ⅛-inch-thick rounds

2 garlic cloves, minced

2 tablespoons vegetable oil

½ teaspoon kosher salt

1. **To prep the miso-glazed peppers:** In a large bowl, mix the vegetable oil, water, miso, and ginger until well combined. Add the shishitos and toss to coat.

2. **To prep the charred lemon peppers:** In a large bowl, combine the shishitos, lemon slices, garlic, vegetable oil, and salt. Toss to coat.

3. **To cook the peppers:** Install a crisper plate in each of the two baskets. Place the miso-glazed peppers in the Zone 1 basket and insert the basket in the unit. Place the peppers with lemons in the Zone 2 basket and insert the basket in the unit.

4. Select Zone 1, select AIR FRY, set the temperature to 390°F, and set the time to 10 minutes. Select MATCH COOK™ to match Zone 2 settings to Zone 1.

5. Press START/PAUSE to begin cooking.

6. When both timers read 4 minutes, press START/PAUSE. Remove both baskets and shake well. Reinsert the baskets and press START/PAUSE to resume cooking.

7. When cooking is complete, serve immediately.

Per serving (miso-glazed): *Calories: 165; Total fat: 14g; Saturated fat: 2g; Carbohydrates: 9g; Fiber: 2g; Protein: 2g; Sodium: 334mg*

Per serving (charred lemon): *Calories: 146; Total fat: 14g; Saturated fat: 2g; Carbohydrates: 6g; Fiber: 2g; Protein: 1g; Sodium: 284mg*

Dried Apple Chips // Dried Banana Chips

SERVES 6

If you're anything like me, you frequently buy more fruit than you can eat before it goes bad. Dehydrating it is a great way to extend its shelf life and turn it into a tasty snack! When apples are dried, their flavor becomes more tart and concentrated. I love adding a sprinkle of cinnamon to make them taste like apple pie. Bananas come out softer and chewier than the freeze-dried bananas you might purchase at the store, with a great intense flavor that reminds me of banana candy.

DAIRY-FREE, GLUTEN-FREE, NUT-FREE, VEGAN

Prep time: 5 minutes
Cook time: 6 to 10 hours

FOR THE APPLE CHIPS

½ teaspoon ground cinnamon

¼ teaspoon ground nutmeg

⅛ teaspoon ground allspice

⅛ teaspoon ground ginger

2 Gala apples, cored and cut into ⅛-inch-thick rings

FOR THE BANANA CHIPS

2 firm-ripe bananas, cut into ¼-inch slices

1. **To prep the apple chips:** In a small bowl, mix the cinnamon, nutmeg, allspice, and ginger until combined. Sprinkle the spice mixture over the apple slices.

2. **To dehydrate the fruit:** Arrange half of the apple slices in a single layer in the Zone 1 basket. It is okay if the edges overlap a bit as they will shrink as they cook. Place a crisper plate on top of the apples. Arrange the remaining apple slices on top of the crisper plate and insert the basket in the unit.

3. Repeat this process with the bananas in the Zone 2 basket and insert the basket in the unit.

4. Select Zone 1, select DEHYDRATE, set the temperature to 135°F, and set the time to 8 hours.

5. Select Zone 2, select DEHYDRATE, set the temperature to 135ºF, and set the time to 10 hours. Select SMART FINISH.™

6. Press START/PAUSE to begin cooking.

7. When both timers read 2 hours, press START/PAUSE. Remove both baskets and check the fruit for doneness; note that juicier fruit will take longer to dry than fruit that starts out drier. Reinsert the basket and press START/PAUSE to continue cooking if necessary.

Per serving (apple): *Calories: 67; Total fat: 0g; Saturated fat: 0g; Carbohydrates: 16g; Fiber: 3g; Protein: 0g; Sodium: 1mg*

Per serving (banana): *Calories: 70; Total fat: 0g; Saturated fat: 0g; Carbohydrates: 18g; Fiber: 2g; Protein: 1g; Sodium: 1mg*

Prep tip: Use 1 teaspoon of store-bought apple pie spice instead of making your own seasoning blend.

Beef Jerky // Pineapple Jerky

SERVES 8

I remember when I was a kid there was a popular infomercial for a dehydrator. I used to watch in awe as the host made her own beef jerky and dried fruit. Flash-forward to years later, and you can only imagine how excited I was to find the Dehydrate function on my air fryer! You can use fresh or canned pineapple for this recipe, but keep in mind that canned pineapple is wetter and might take longer to fully dehydrate.

NUT-FREE, DAIRY-FREE

Prep time: 10 minutes, plus 8 hours to marinate
Cook time: 6 to 12 hours

FOR THE BEEF JERKY

½ **cup reduced-sodium soy sauce**

¼ **cup pineapple juice**

1 **tablespoon dark brown sugar**

1 **tablespoon Worcestershire sauce**

½ **teaspoon smoked paprika**

¼ **teaspoon freshly ground black pepper**

¼ **teaspoon red pepper flakes**

1 **pound beef bottom round, trimmed of excess fat, cut into ¼-inch-thick slices**

FOR THE PINEAPPLE JERKY

1 **pound pineapple, cut into ⅛-inch-thick rounds, pat dry**

1 **teaspoon chili powder (optional)**

1. **To prep the beef jerky:** In a large zip-top bag, combine the soy sauce, pineapple juice, brown sugar, Worcestershire sauce, smoked paprika, black pepper, and red pepper flakes.

2. Add the beef slices, seal the bag, and toss to coat the meat in the marinade. Refrigerate overnight or for at least 8 hours.

3. Remove the beef slices and discard the marinade. Using a paper towel, pat the slices dry to remove excess marinade.

4. **To prep the pineapple jerky:** Sprinkle the pineapple with chili powder (if using).

5. **To dehydrate the jerky:** Arrange half of the beef slices in a single layer in the Zone 1 basket, making sure they do not overlap. Place a crisper plate on top of the beef slices and arrange the remaining slices in a single layer on top of the crisper plate. Insert the basket in the unit.

6. Repeat this process with the pineapple in the Zone 2 basket and insert the basket in the unit.

7. Select Zone 1, select DEHYDRATE, set the temperature to 150ºF, and set the time to 8 hours.

8. Select Zone 2, select DEHYDRATE, set the temperature to 135ºF, and set the time to 12 hours.

9. Press START/PAUSE to begin cooking.

10. When the Zone 1 timer reads 2 hours, press START/PAUSE. Remove the basket and check the beef jerky for doneness. If necessary, reinsert the basket and press START/PAUSE to resume cooking.

Per serving (beef): *Calories: 171; Total fat: 6.5g; Saturated fat: 2g; Carbohydrates: 2g; Fiber: 0g; Protein: 25g; Sodium: 369mg*

Per serving (pineapple): *Calories: 57; Total fat: 0g; Saturated fat: 0g; Carbohydrates: 15g; Fiber: 1.5g; Protein: 0g; Sodium: 1mg*

Roasted Tomato Bruschetta with Toasty Garlic Bread

SERVES 4

This Italian-inspired recipe is perfect as an appetizer or as a simple snack. Roasting the tomatoes brings out their natural sweetness, and the balsamic vinegar gives it a delicious tang. You'll love the way the sweet tomato topping pairs with crispy garlic bread and creamy ricotta cheese.

NUT-FREE, VEGETARIAN

Prep time: 10 minutes
Cook time: 12 minutes

FOR THE ROASTED TOMATOES
- 10 ounces cherry tomatoes, cut in half
- 1 tablespoon balsamic vinegar
- 1 tablespoon olive oil
- ¼ teaspoon kosher salt
- ¼ teaspoon freshly ground black pepper

FOR THE GARLIC BREAD
- 4 slices crusty Italian bread
- 1 tablespoon olive oil
- 3 garlic cloves, minced
- ¼ teaspoon Italian seasoning

FOR THE BRUSCHETTA
- ¼ cup loosely packed fresh basil, thinly sliced
- ½ cup part-skim ricotta cheese

1. **To prep the tomatoes:** In a small bowl, combine the tomatoes, vinegar, oil, salt, and black pepper.

2. **To prep the garlic bread:** Brush one side of each bread slice with the oil. Sprinkle with the garlic and Italian seasoning.

3. **To cook the tomatoes and garlic bread:** Install a broil rack in the Zone 1 basket (without the crisper plate installed). Place the tomatoes on the rack in the basket and insert the basket in the unit.

4. Place 2 slices of bread in the Zone 2 basket and insert the basket in the unit.

5. Select Zone 1, select AIR BROIL, set the temperature to 450ºF, and set the time to 12 minutes.

6. Select Zone 2, select AIR FRY, set the temperature to 360ºF, and set the time to 10 minutes. Select SMART FINISH.™

7. Press START/PAUSE to begin cooking.

8. When the Zone 2 timer reads 5 minutes, press START/PAUSE. Remove the basket and transfer the garlic bread to a cutting board. Place the remaining 2 slices of garlic bread in the basket. Reinsert the basket in the unit and press START/PAUSE to resume cooking.

9. **To assemble the bruschetta:** When cooking is complete, add the basil to the tomatoes and stir to combine. Spread 2 tablespoons of ricotta onto each slice of garlic bread and top with the tomatoes. Serve warm or at room temperature.

Per serving: Calories: 212; Total fat: 11g; Saturated fat: 2.5g; Carbohydrates: 22g; Fiber: 1.5g; Protein: 6g; Sodium: 286mg

Prep tip: You can use frozen garlic bread instead of making your own. Place the frozen bread in the air fryer butter-side up and AIR FRY at 370°F for 8 minutes, flipping halfway through.

Buffalo Wings // Honey-Garlic Wings

SERVES 6

Chicken wings were one of the first things I made when I got an air fryer, and I immediately knew it was worth every cent. The skin gets super crisp, but the meat inside stays nice and juicy. Whether you like your wings spicy or sweet, you can't go wrong with this recipe—you get both! Seasoning the wings with dry spices in addition to the sauce means you get extra flavor in every bite.

DAIRY-FREE, NUT-FREE

Prep time: 10 minutes
Cook time: 40 minutes

FOR THE BUFFALO WINGS

2 pounds chicken wings

¼ teaspoon kosher salt

¼ teaspoon freshly ground black pepper

¼ teaspoon paprika

1 tablespoon vegetable oil

⅓ cup Buffalo wing sauce

FOR THE HONEY-GARLIC WINGS

2 pounds chicken wings

2 tablespoons all-purpose flour

½ teaspoon garlic powder

1 tablespoon vegetable oil

¼ cup honey

2 tablespoons reduced-sodium soy sauce

½ teaspoon ground ginger (optional)

1. **To prep the Buffalo wings:** In a large bowl, combine the wings, salt, black pepper, and paprika and toss to coat the wings with the seasonings. Drizzle with the oil.

2. **To prep the honey-garlic wings:** In another large bowl, combine the wings, flour, and garlic powder and toss to coat the wings. Drizzle with the oil.

3. In a small bowl, whisk together the honey, soy sauce, and ginger (if using). Set the honey-soy sauce aside.

CONTINUED >

Prep tip: Buffalo wing sauce is easy to find in most grocery stores and makes delicious wings so easy. If you prefer to make your own, mix your favorite hot sauce with melted butter to taste.

4. To cook the wings: Install a crisper plate in each of the two baskets. Place the Buffalo wings in the Zone 1 basket and insert the basket in the unit. Place the honey-garlic wings in the Zone 2 basket and insert the basket in the unit.

5. Select Zone 1, select AIR FRY, set the temperature to 390°F, and set the time to 40 minutes. Select MATCH COOK™ to match Zone 2 settings to Zone 1.

6. Press START/PAUSE to begin cooking.

7. When both timers read 8 minutes, press START/PAUSE. Remove the Zone 1 basket, drizzle the Buffalo sauce over the wings, and shake to coat the wings with the sauce. Reinsert the basket. Remove the Zone 2 basket, drizzle the honey-soy sauce over the wings, and shake to coat the wings with the sauce. Reinsert the basket. Press START/PAUSE to resume cooking.

8. When cooking is complete, the wings will be golden brown and cooked through. Use silicone-tipped tongs to transfer the wings to a serving plate. Serve warm.

Per serving (Buffalo): *Calories: 399; Total fat: 28g; Saturated fat: 7.5g; Carbohydrates: 0g; Fiber: 0g; Protein: 34g; Sodium: 1,049mg*

Per serving (honey-garlic): *Calories: 509; Total fat: 28g; Saturated fat: 7.5g; Carbohydrates: 27g; Fiber: 0g; Protein: 35g; Sodium: 523mg*

Bacon-Wrapped Dates //
Bacon-Wrapped Scallops

SERVES 6

Whether you're hosting a game-day gathering or a formal dinner, this assortment of bacon-wrapped scallops and bacon-wrapped dates will be sure to wow the guests at your next gathering. The salty bacon gets super crispy in the air fryer and pairs so nicely with the sweet, succulent scallops and dates.

DAIRY-FREE, GLUTEN-FREE, NUT-FREE

Prep time: 10 minutes
Cook time: 12 minutes

FOR THE SCALLOPS
6 slices bacon, halved crosswise

12 large sea scallops, patted dry

FOR THE DATES
4 slices bacon, cut into thirds

12 pitted dates

1. **To prep the dates:** Wrap each piece of bacon around a date and secure with a toothpick.

2. **To cook the dates and the bacon for the scallops:** Install a crisper plate in each of the two baskets. Place the bacon for the scallops in the Zone 1 basket in a single layer and insert the basket in the unit. Place the bacon-wrapped dates in the Zone 2 basket in a single layer and insert the basket in the unit.

3. Select Zone 1, select AIR FRY, set the temperature to 400°F, and set the time to 12 minutes.

4. Select Zone 2, select AIR FRY, set the temperature to 360°F, and set the time to 10 minutes. Select SMART FINISH.™

5. Press START/PAUSE to begin cooking.

CONTINUED >

6. When the Zone 1 timer reads 9 minutes, press START/PAUSE. Remove the basket from the unit. Wrap each piece of bacon around a scallop and secure with a toothpick. Place the bacon-wrapped scallops in the basket. Reinsert the basket and press START/PAUSE to resume cooking.

7. When the Zone 1 timer reads 4 minutes, press START/PAUSE. Remove the basket and use silicone-tipped tongs to flip the scallops. Reinsert the basket and press START/PAUSE to resume cooking.

8. When cooking is complete, the scallops will be opaque and the bacon around both the scallops and dates will be crisp. Arrange the bacon-wrapped scallops and dates on a serving platter. Serve warm.

Per serving (4 dates): *Calories: 191; Total fat: 2.5g; Saturated fat: 1g; Carbohydrates: 39g; Fiber: 4g; Protein: 3g; Sodium: 115mg*

Per serving (4 scallops): *Calories: 88; Total fat: 4g; Saturated fat: 1.5g; Carbohydrates: 2g; Fiber: 0g; Protein: 10g; Sodium: 408mg*

Crab Rangoon Dip with Crispy Wonton Strips

Your family will go crazy over this bubbling hot dip that tastes like the inside of a crab rangoon. Serve the dip with plenty of crispy air-fried wonton strips for dipping! You can cook the wonton strips in multiple layers, but be sure to give them a firm shake several times during the cooking process to keep them from sticking together as they air fry.

NUT-FREE

Prep time: 10 minutes
Cook time: 15 minutes

FOR THE DIP

1 (6-ounce) can pink crab, drained

8 ounces (16 tablespoons) cream cheese, at room temperature

½ cup sour cream

1 tablespoon chopped scallions

½ teaspoon garlic powder

1 teaspoon Worcestershire sauce

¼ teaspoon kosher salt

1 cup shredded part-skim mozzarella cheese

FOR THE WONTON STRIPS

12 wonton wrappers

1 tablespoon olive oil

¼ teaspoon kosher salt

1. **To prep the dip:** In a medium bowl, mix the crab, cream cheese, sour cream, scallions, garlic powder, Worcestershire sauce, and salt until smooth.

2. **To prep the wonton strips:** Brush both sides of the wonton wrappers with the oil and sprinkle with salt. Cut the wonton wrappers into ¾-inch-wide strips.

3. **To cook the dip and strips:** Pour the dip into the Zone 1 basket, top with the mozzarella cheese, and insert the basket in the unit. Install a crisper plate in the Zone 2 basket, add the wonton strips, and insert the basket in the unit.

4. Select Zone 1, select BAKE, set the temperature to 330ºF, and set the time to 15 minutes.

5. Select Zone 2, select AIR FRY, set the temperature to 350°F, and set the time to 6 minutes. Select SMART FINISH.™

6. Press START/PAUSE to begin cooking.

7. When the Zone 2 timer reads 4 minutes, press START/PAUSE. Remove the basket and shake well to redistribute the wonton strips. Reinsert the basket and press START/PAUSE to resume cooking.

8. When the Zone 2 timer reads 2 minutes, press START/PAUSE. Remove the basket and shake well to redistribute the wonton strips. Reinsert the basket and press START/PAUSE to resume cooking.

9. When cooking is complete, the dip will be bubbling and golden brown on top and the wonton strips will be crunchy. Serve warm.

Per serving: *Calories: 315; Total fat: 23g; Saturated fat: 12g; Carbohydrates: 14g; Fiber: 0.5g; Protein: 14g; Sodium: 580mg*

Jalapeño Popper Dip with Tortilla Chips

SERVES 6

This dip is perfect for game day or any casual gathering. Pickled jalapeños add a delicious kick, while the cream cheese and sour cream tone down the heat. Serve with crispy tortilla chips for a fun and easy snack based on the popular jalapeño popper appetizer.

NUT-FREE, VEGETARIAN

Prep time: 10 minutes
Cook time: 15 minutes

FOR THE DIP

8 ounces cream cheese, at room temperature

½ cup sour cream

1 cup shredded Cheddar cheese

¼ cup shredded Parmesan cheese

¼ cup roughly chopped pickled jalapeños

½ teaspoon kosher salt

½ cup panko bread crumbs

2 tablespoons olive oil

½ teaspoon dried parsley

FOR THE TORTILLA CHIPS

10 corn tortillas

2 tablespoons fresh lime juice

1 tablespoon olive oil

½ teaspoon kosher salt

1. **To prep the dip:** In a medium bowl, mix the cream cheese, sour cream, Cheddar, Parmesan, jalapeños, and salt until smooth.

2. In a small bowl, combine the panko, olive oil, and parsley.

3. Pour the dip into a 14-ounce ramekin and top with the panko mixture.

4. **To prep the chips:** Brush both sides of each tortilla with lime juice, then with oil. Sprinkle with the salt. Using a sharp knife or a pizza cutter, cut each tortilla into 4 wedges.

5. To cook the dip and chips: Install a crisper plate in each of the two baskets. Place the ramekin of dip in the Zone 1 basket and insert the basket in the unit. Layer the tortillas in the Zone 2 basket and insert the basket in the unit.

6. Select Zone 1, select BAKE, set the temperature to 350ºF, and set the time to 15 minutes.

7. Select Zone 2, select AIR FRY, set the temperature to 375ºF, and set the time to 5 minutes. Select SMART FINISH.™

8. Press START/PAUSE to begin cooking.

9. When the Zone 2 timer reads 3 minutes, press START/PAUSE. Remove the basket from the unit and give the basket a good shake to redistribute the chips. Reinsert the basket and press START/PAUSE to resume cooking.

10. When cooking is complete, the dip will be bubbling and golden brown and the chips will be crispy. Serve warm.

Per serving: Calories: 406; Total fat: 31g; Saturated fat: 14g; Carbohydrates: 22g; Fiber: 1g; Protein: 11g; Sodium: 539mg

Chili-Lime Crispy Chickpeas // Pizza-Seasoned Crispy Chickpeas

SERVES 6

Move over, potato chips—there's a new snack in town, and it's packing some serious flavor. Seasoned with all the right herbs and spices, these crispy chickpeas are perfect for satisfying all of your snack cravings.

GLUTEN-FREE, NUT-FREE, VEGETARIAN

Prep time: 5 minutes
Cook time: 20 minutes

FOR THE CHILI-LIME CHICKPEAS

1½ cups canned chickpeas, rinsed and drained

¼ cup fresh lime juice

1 tablespoon olive oil

1½ teaspoons chili powder

½ teaspoon kosher salt

FOR THE PIZZA-SEASONED CHICKPEAS

1½ cups canned chickpeas, rinsed and drained

1 tablespoon olive oil

1 tablespoon grated Parmesan cheese

½ teaspoon dried basil

½ teaspoon dried oregano

½ teaspoon kosher salt

¼ teaspoon onion powder

¼ teaspoon garlic powder

¼ teaspoon fennel seeds

¼ teaspoon dried thyme

¼ teaspoon red pepper flakes (optional)

1. **To prep the chili-lime chickpeas:** In a small bowl, mix the chickpeas, lime juice, olive oil, chili powder, and salt until the chickpeas are well coated.

2. **To prep the pizza-seasoned chickpeas:** In a small bowl, mix the chickpeas, olive oil, Parmesan, basil, oregano, salt, onion powder, garlic powder, fennel, thyme, and red pepper flakes (if using) until the chickpeas are well coated.

3. **To cook the chickpeas:** Install a crisper plate in each of the two baskets. Place the chili-lime chickpeas in the Zone 1 basket and insert the basket in the unit. Place the pizza-seasoned chickpeas in the Zone 2 basket and insert the basket in the unit.

4. Select Zone 1, select AIR FRY, set the temperature to 375°F, and set the time to 20 minutes. Select MATCH COOK™ to match Zone 2 settings to Zone 1.

5. Press START/PAUSE to begin cooking.

6. When both timers read 10 minutes, press START/PAUSE. Remove both baskets and give each basket a shake to redistribute the chickpeas. Reinsert both baskets and press START/PAUSE to resume cooking.

7. When both timers read 5 minutes, press START/PAUSE. Remove both baskets and give each basket a good shake again. Reinsert both baskets and press START/PAUSE to resume cooking.

8. When cooking is complete, the chickpeas will be crisp and golden brown. Serve warm or at room temperature.

Per serving (chili-lime): *Calories: 145; Total fat: 6.5g; Saturated fat: 0.5g; Carbohydrates: 17g; Fiber: 4.5g; Protein: 5g; Sodium: 348mg*

Per serving (pizza-seasoned): *Calories: 152; Total fat: 7g; Saturated fat: 1g; Carbohydrates: 17g; Fiber: 4.5g; Protein: 6g; Sodium: 378mg*

Prep tip: You can use a prepared chili-lime seasoning blend instead of making your own. You'll need about 2 teaspoons of seasoning per batch of chickpeas.

"Fried" Ravioli with Zesty Marinara

SERVES 6

I've been making fried ravioli for years, but only recently started making them in the air fryer. They come out surprisingly well and you don't need to boil the ravioli first. The bread crumbs get crisp and golden brown in the air fryer without the mess of traditional deep-frying. I serve these crispy treats with a simple home-made marinara sauce made right in my Ninja® Foodi.® If you love fried cheese, you won't want to miss this recipe.

NUT-FREE, VEGETARIAN

Prep time: 15 minutes
Cook time: 20 minutes

FOR THE RAVIOLI
¼ **cup all-purpose flour**
1 large egg
1 tablespoon water
⅔ **cup Italian-style bread crumbs**
1 pound frozen cheese ravioli, thawed
Nonstick cooking spray

FOR THE MARINARA
1 (28-ounce) can chunky crushed tomatoes with basil and oregano
1 tablespoon unsalted butter
2 garlic cloves, minced
¼ **teaspoon kosher salt**
¼ **teaspoon red pepper flakes**

1. **To prep the ravioli:** Set up a breading station with three small shallow bowls. Put the flour in the first bowl. In the second bowl, beat the egg and water. Place the bread crumbs in the third bowl.

2. Bread the ravioli in this order: First dip them into the flour, coating both sides. Then dip into the beaten egg. Finally, coat them in the bread crumbs, gently pressing the crumbs into the ravioli to help them stick.

3. Mist both sides of the ravioli generously with cooking spray.

4. **To prep the marinara:** In the Zone 2 basket, combine the crushed tomatoes, butter, garlic, salt, and red pepper flakes.

5. To cook the ravioli and sauce: Install a crisper plate in the Zone 1 basket and add the ravioli to the basket. Insert the basket in the unit. Insert the Zone 2 basket in the unit.

6. Select Zone 1, select AIR FRY, set the temperature to 390ºF, and set the time to 20 minutes.

7. Select Zone 2, select BAKE, set the temperature to 350ºF, and set the time to 15 minutes. Select SMART FINISH.™

8. Press START/PAUSE to begin cooking.

9. When the Zone 1 timer reads 7 minutes, press START/PAUSE. Remove the basket and shake to redistribute the ravioli. Reinsert the basket and press START/PAUSE to resume cooking.

10. When cooking is complete, the breading will be crisp and golden brown. Transfer the ravioli to a plate and the marinara to a bowl. Serve hot.

Per serving: Calories: 282; Total fat: 8g; Saturated fat: 3g; Carbohydrates: 39g; Fiber: 4.5g; Protein: 13g; Sodium: 369mg

Prep tip: Using seasoned bread crumbs and tomatoes means less time digging through your spice rack when it's time to cook.

Barbecue Chicken Drumsticks with Crispy Kale Chips, *page 74*

4

Poultry

Lemon-Pepper Chicken Thighs with Buttery Roasted Radishes

SERVES 4

Lemon pepper is a great way to jazz up chicken for dinner. These juicy thighs are simple and delicious, and the Ninja® Foodi® Air Fryer makes the skin so crispy! Buttery roasted radishes are a great low-carb side dish that rounds out this meal nicely. The radishes have a starchy, potato-like texture and a peppery, slightly vegetal flavor.

GLUTEN-FREE, NUT-FREE

Prep time: 5 minutes
Cook time: 28 minutes

FOR THE CHICKEN
4 bone-in, skin-on chicken thighs (6 ounces each)
1 teaspoon olive oil

2 teaspoons lemon pepper
¼ teaspoon kosher salt

FOR THE RADISHES
1 bunch radishes (greens removed), halved through the stem
1 teaspoon olive oil
¼ teaspoon kosher salt

¼ teaspoon freshly ground black pepper
1 tablespoon unsalted butter, cut into small pieces
2 tablespoons chopped fresh parsley

1. **To prep the chicken:** Brush both sides of the chicken thighs with olive oil, then season with lemon pepper and salt.

2. **To prep the radishes:** In a large bowl, combine the radishes, olive oil, salt, and black pepper. Stir well to coat the radishes.

3. **To cook the chicken and radishes:** Install a crisper plate in each of the two baskets. Place the chicken skin-side up in the Zone 1 basket and insert the basket in the unit. Place the radishes in the Zone 2 basket and insert the basket in the unit.

4. Select Zone 1, select AIR FRY, set the temperature to 390ºF, and set the time to 28 minutes.

5. Select Zone 2, select ROAST, set the temperature to 400°F, and set the time to 15 minutes. Select SMART FINISH.™

6. Press START/PAUSE to begin cooking.

7. When the Zone 2 timer reads 5 minutes, press START/PAUSE. Remove the basket, scatter the butter pieces over the radishes, and reinsert the basket. Press START/PAUSE to resume cooking.

8. When cooking is complete, the chicken should be cooked through (an instant-read thermometer should read at least 165°F) and the radishes will be soft. Stir the parsley into the radishes and serve.

Per serving: Calories: 271; Total fat: 29g; Saturated fat: 6g; Carbohydrates: 5g; Fiber: 1g; Protein: 23g; Sodium: 246mg

Super swap: These chicken thighs also pair well with Broiled Zucchini and Cherry Tomatoes (page 83), Lemon-Feta Baby Potatoes (page 126), and Honey-Roasted Carrots (page 146).

Barbecue Chicken Drumsticks with Crispy Kale Chips

SERVES 4

These baked drumsticks have a double dose of smoky barbecue flavor, thanks to a simple dry rub and store-bought barbecue sauce. Paired with a healthy serving of garlicky kale chips, this meal is comfort food at its finest.

DAIRY-FREE, GLUTEN-FREE, NUT-FREE

Prep time: 10 minutes
Cook time: 20 minutes

FOR THE DRUMSTICKS

1 tablespoon chili powder

2 teaspoons smoked paprika

¼ teaspoon kosher salt

¼ teaspoon garlic powder

¼ teaspoon freshly ground black pepper

2 teaspoons dark brown sugar

4 chicken drumsticks

1 cup barbecue sauce (your favorite)

FOR THE KALE CHIPS

5 cups kale, stems and midribs removed, if needed

½ teaspoon garlic powder

½ teaspoon kosher salt

¼ teaspoon freshly ground black pepper

1. **To prep the drumsticks:** In a small bowl, combine the chili powder, smoked paprika, salt, garlic powder, black pepper, and brown sugar. Rub the spice mixture all over the chicken.

2. **To cook the chicken and kale chips:** Install a crisper plate in each of the two baskets. Add the chicken drumsticks to the Zone 1 basket and insert the basket in the unit. Add the kale to the Zone 2 basket, sprinkle the kale with the garlic powder, salt, and black pepper and insert the basket in the unit.

3. Select Zone 1, select BAKE, set the temperature to 390°F, and set the time to 20 minutes.

4. Select Zone 2, select AIR FRY, set the temperature to 300ºF, and set the time to 15 minutes. Select SMART FINISH.™

5. Press START/PAUSE to begin cooking.

6. When the Zone 1 timer reads 5 minutes, press START/PAUSE. Remove the basket and brush the drumsticks with the barbecue sauce. Reinsert the basket and press START/PAUSE to resume cooking.

7. When cooking is complete, the chicken should be cooked through (an instant-read thermometer should read 165ºF) and the kale chips will be crispy. Serve hot.

Per serving: Calories: 335; Total fat: 11g; Saturated fat: 3g; Carbohydrates: 31g; Fiber: 1.5g; Protein: 26g; Sodium: 1,045mg

Super swap: Try these chicken drumsticks with Seasoned Potato Wedges (page 155), Sweet Potato Fries (page 157), or Baked Macaroni and Cheese (page 148).

Chicken Fajitas with Street Corn

SERVES 4

These fajitas are easy, delicious, and filling. Thinly sliced chicken breast cooks quickly and I love the way the peppers and onions brown and caramelize in the air fryer, adding amazing flavor to the dish. It's so perfect to pair them with street corn for a fun meal that you can eat entirely by hand. Feel free to use frozen ears of corn if corn is out of season. Cotija cheese is traditional, but feta is more readily available and provides the same creamy texture and salty flavor.

NUT-FREE

Prep time: 10 minutes
Cook time: 20 minutes

FOR THE FAJITAS

1½ pounds boneless, skinless chicken breasts, cut into strips

2 bell peppers (red, orange, yellow, or a combination), sliced Into ½-inch-wide strips

1 small red onion, sliced

1 tablespoon vegetable oil

2 teaspoons chili powder

1 teaspoon ground cumin

1 teaspoon kosher salt

½ teaspoon freshly ground black pepper

½ teaspoon paprika

¼ cup fresh cilantro, chopped

Juice of 1 lime

8 (6-inch) flour tortillas

FOR THE CORN

¼ cup mayonnaise

¼ cup sour cream

¼ cup crumbled Cotija or feta cheese

2 tablespoons chopped fresh cilantro

1 teaspoon minced garlic

½ teaspoon chili powder

4 ears corn, husked

1. **To prep the fajitas:** In a large bowl, combine the chicken, bell peppers, onion, oil, chili powder, cumin, salt, black pepper, and paprika and toss to coat.

2. **To prep the corn:** In a shallow dish, combine the mayonnaise, sour cream, cheese, cilantro, garlic, and chili powder. Mix well and set aside.

3. **To cook the fajitas and corn:** Install a crisper plate in each of the two baskets. Place the fajita filling in the Zone 1 basket and insert the basket in the unit. Place the corn ears in the Zone 2 basket and insert the basket in the unit.

4. Select Zone 1, select AIR FRY, set the temperature to 390°F, and set the time to 20 minutes.

5. Select Zone 2, select AIR BROIL, set the temperature to 450°F, and set the time to 12 minutes. Select SMART FINISH.™

6. Press START/PAUSE to begin cooking.

7. When both timers read 6 minutes, press START/PAUSE. Remove the Zone 1 basket, shake to redistribute the fajita filling, and reinsert the basket. Remove the Zone 2 basket and use silicone-tipped tongs to flip the corn. Reinsert the basket and press START/PAUSE to resume cooking.

8. When cooking is complete, the chicken will be fully cooked and the vegetables will be slightly charred.

9. Mix the cilantro and lime juice into the fajita filling. Divide the filling among the tortillas. Roll the corn in the mayonnaise and cheese mixture to coat. Serve hot.

Per serving: Calories: 705; Total fat: 29g; Saturated fat: 8g; Carbohydrates: 60g; Fiber: 5g; Protein: 51g; Sodium: 1,155mg

Super swap: Try these fajitas with Mexican Rice (page 116), Buttery Roasted Radishes (page 72), or Crispy Kale Chips (page 74).

Sweet-and-Sour Chicken with Pineapple Cauliflower Rice

SERVES 4

Sweet-and-sour chicken is one of those dishes that I was kind of obsessed with as a kid. I loved the sweet and tangy sauce so much! This version has that same flavor profile but is easy to make in your Ninja® Foodi® 2-Basket Air Fryer. The chicken is paired with pineapple cauliflower rice to really highlight the sweet, tropical flavor of this meal.

DAIRY-FREE, NUT-FREE

Prep time: 15 minutes
Cook time: 30 minutes

FOR THE CHICKEN

¼ cup cornstarch, plus 2 teaspoons

¼ teaspoon kosher salt

2 large eggs

1 tablespoon sesame oil

1½ pounds boneless, skinless chicken breasts, cut into 1-inch pieces

Nonstick cooking spray

6 tablespoons ketchup

¾ cup apple cider vinegar

1½ tablespoons soy sauce

1 tablespoon sugar

FOR THE CAULIFLOWER RICE

1 cup finely diced fresh pineapple

1 red bell pepper, thinly sliced

1 small red onion, thinly sliced

1 tablespoon vegetable oil

2 cups frozen cauliflower rice, thawed

2 tablespoons soy sauce

1 teaspoon sesame oil

2 scallions, sliced

1. To prep the chicken: Set up a breading station with two small shallow bowls. Combine ¼ cup of cornstarch and the salt in the first bowl. In the second bowl, beat the eggs with the sesame oil.

2. Dip the chicken pieces in the cornstarch mixture to coat, then into the egg mixture, then back into the cornstarch mixture to coat. Mist the coated pieces with cooking spray.

3. In a small bowl, whisk together the ketchup, vinegar, soy sauce, sugar, and remaining 2 teaspoons of cornstarch.

4. **To prep the cauliflower rice:** Blot the pineapple dry with a paper towel. In a large bowl, combine the pineapple, bell pepper, onion, and vegetable oil.

5. **To cook the chicken and cauliflower rice:** Install a crisper plate in each of the two baskets. Place the chicken in the Zone 1 basket and insert the basket in the unit. Place a piece of aluminum foil over the crisper plate in the Zone 2 basket and add the pineapple mixture. Insert the basket in the unit.

6. Select Zone 1, select AIR FRY, set the temperature to 400°F, and set the time to 30 minutes.

7. Select Zone 2, select AIR BROIL, set the temperature to 450°F, and set the time to 12 minutes. Select SMART FINISH.™

8. Press START/PAUSE to begin cooking.

9. When the Zone 2 timer reads 4 minutes, press START/PAUSE. Remove the basket and stir in the cauliflower rice, soy sauce, and sesame oil. Reinsert the basket and press START/PAUSE to resume cooking.

10. When cooking is complete, the chicken will be golden brown and cooked through and the rice warmed through. Stir the scallions into the rice and serve.

Super swap: This sweet-and-sour chicken also pairs well with Seasoned Rice (page 129) or Roasted Green Beans and Shallots (page 135).

Per serving: Calories: 457; Total fat: 17g; Saturated fat: 2.5g; Carbohydrates: 31g; Fiber: 2.5g; Protein: 43g; Sodium: 1,526mg

Orange Chicken with Roasted Snap Peas and Scallions

SERVES 4

Add a little sweetness to your life with this delicious orange chicken recipe. The chicken is coated with a cornstarch batter that transforms into light and crispy bites in the air fryer, while fresh orange juice and orange zest add tons of bright citrusy flavor to the sauce. I love serving this with roasted snap peas and scallions for a nutritious and tasty crunch.

DAIRY-FREE, NUT-FREE

Prep time: 15 minutes
Cook time: 30 minutes

FOR THE CHICKEN
- ⅓ cup all-purpose flour
- 2 large eggs
- ⅓ cup cornstarch, plus 2 tablespoons
- 1½ pounds boneless, skinless chicken breasts, cut into 1-inch pieces
- Nonstick cooking spray
- 2 tablespoons grated orange zest
- 1 cup freshly squeezed orange juice
- ¼ cup granulated sugar
- 2 tablespoons rice vinegar
- 2 tablespoons soy sauce
- ¼ teaspoon minced fresh ginger
- ¼ teaspoon grated garlic

FOR THE SNAP PEAS
- 8 ounces snap peas
- 1 tablespoon vegetable oil
- ½ teaspoon minced garlic
- ½ teaspoon grated fresh ginger
- ¼ teaspoon kosher salt
- ¼ teaspoon freshly ground black pepper
- 4 scallions, thinly sliced

1. **To prep the chicken:** Set up a breading station with three small shallow bowls. Place the flour in the first bowl. In the second bowl, beat the eggs. Place ⅓ cup of cornstarch in the third bowl.

2. Bread the chicken pieces in this order: First, dip them into the flour to coat. Then, dip into the beaten egg. Finally, add them to the cornstarch, coating all sides. Mist the breaded chicken with cooking spray.

3. In a small bowl, whisk together the orange zest, orange juice, sugar, vinegar, soy sauce, ginger, garlic, and remaining 2 tablespoons of cornstarch. Set orange sauce aside.

4. To prep the snap peas: In a large bowl, combine the snap peas, oil, garlic, ginger, salt, and black pepper. Toss to coat.

5. To cook the chicken and snap peas: Install a crisper plate in the Zone 1 basket. Add the chicken to the basket and insert the basket in the unit. Place the snap peas in the Zone 2 basket and insert the basket in the unit.

6. Select Zone 1, select AIR FRY, set the temperature to 400°F, and set the time to 30 minutes.

7. Select Zone 2, select ROAST, set the temperature to 375°F, and set the time to 12 minutes. Select SMART FINISH.™

8. Press START/PAUSE to begin cooking.

9. When the Zone 1 timer reads 15 minutes, press START/PAUSE. Remove the basket and shake to redistribute the chicken. Reinsert the basket and press START/PAUSE to resume cooking.

10. When the Zone 1 timer reads 5 minutes, press START/PAUSE. Remove the basket and pour the reserved orange sauce over the chicken. Reinsert the basket and press START/PAUSE to resume cooking.

11. When cooking is complete, the chicken and vegetables will be cooked through. Stir the scallions into the snap peas. Serve hot.

Super swap: Try this orange chicken with Pineapple Cauliflower Rice (page 78), Roasted Bok Choy (page 160), or Miso-Glazed Shishito Peppers (page 48).

Per serving: Calories: 473; Total fat: 13g; Saturated fat: 2g; Carbohydrates: 43g; Fiber: 2g; Protein: 44g; Sodium: 803mg

Goat Cheese–Stuffed Chicken Breast with Broiled Zucchini and Cherry Tomatoes

SERVES 4

I have a major weakness for goat cheese. It's so tangy and creamy, and it makes the perfect stuffing for chicken breasts. This recipe is chock-full of fresh flavor, highlighted by the broiled zucchini and tomatoes. The vegetables are a simple side dish, but it's one of my favorites.

GLUTEN-FREE, NUT-FREE

Prep time: 10 minutes
Cook time: 25 minutes

FOR THE STUFFED CHICKEN BREASTS

2 ounces soft goat cheese

1 tablespoon minced fresh parsley

½ teaspoon minced garlic

4 boneless, skinless chicken breasts (6 ounces each)

1 tablespoon vegetable oil

½ teaspoon Italian seasoning

½ teaspoon kosher salt

½ teaspoon freshly ground black pepper

FOR THE ZUCCHINI AND TOMATOES

1 pound zucchini, diced

1 cup cherry tomatoes, halved

1 tablespoon vegetable oil

½ teaspoon kosher salt

¼ teaspoon freshly ground black pepper

1. **To prep the stuffed chicken breasts:** In a small bowl, combine the goat cheese, parsley, and garlic. Mix well.

2. Cut a deep slit into the fatter side of each chicken breast to create a pocket (taking care to not go all the way through). Stuff each breast with the goat cheese mixture. Use a toothpick to secure the opening of the chicken, if needed.

3. Brush the outside of the chicken breasts with the oil and season with the Italian seasoning, salt, and black pepper.

4. **To prep the zucchini and tomatoes:** In a large bowl, combine the zucchini, tomatoes, and oil. Mix to coat. Season with salt and black pepper. CONTINUED >

Goat Cheese–Stuffed Chicken Breast with Broiled Zucchini and Cherry Tomatoes continued

Variation: Don't feel like chicken? This recipe is also fantastic when made with rolled stuffed flank steak. Add some chopped sun-dried tomatoes to the filling for even more savory flavor. Spread the filling over the top of the steak, then roll it. Secure it with toothpicks, if needed.

Super swap: Pair this cheese-stuffed chicken with Buttery Roasted Radishes (page 72) or Roasted Asparagus and Mushroom Medley (page 112).

5. To cook the chicken and vegetables: Install a crisper plate in each of the two baskets. Insert a broil rack in the Zone 2 basket over the crisper plate. Place the chicken in the Zone 1 basket and insert the basket in the unit. Place the vegetables on the broiler rack in the Zone 2 basket and insert the basket in the unit.

6. Select Zone 1, select AIR FRY, set the temperature to 390°F, and set the time to 25 minutes.

7. Select Zone 2, select AIR BROIL, set the temperature to 450°F, and set the time to 10 minutes. Select SMART FINISH.™

8. Press START/PAUSE to begin cooking.

9. When cooking is complete, the chicken will be golden brown and cooked through (an instant-read thermometer should read 165°F) and the zucchini will be soft and slightly charred. Serve hot.

Per serving: *Calories: 330; Total fat: 15g; Saturated fat: 4g; Carbohydrates: 5g; Fiber: 1.5g; Protein: 42g; Sodium: 409mg*

Chicken Parmesan with Roasted Lemon-Parmesan Broccoli

SERVES 4

Crispy chicken Parmesan is so delicious, but it can be tricky to make on the stovetop. The air fryer solves that problem by turning out a perfectly crisp and golden chicken cutlet that's still juicy inside. Once the chicken is crisp and cooked through, it only takes a few minutes to warm the sauce and melt the cheese on top. I love pairing this with roasted broccoli doused with a lemony vinaigrette to complement the richness of the meal.

NUT-FREE

Prep time: 15 minutes
Cook time: 18 minutes

FOR THE CHICKEN PARMESAN

- 2 tablespoons all-purpose flour
- 2 large eggs
- 1 cup panko bread crumbs
- 2 tablespoons grated Parmesan cheese
- 2 teaspoons Italian seasoning
- 4 thin-sliced chicken cutlets (4 ounces each)
- 2 tablespoons vegetable oil
- ½ cup marinara sauce
- ½ cup shredded part-skim mozzarella cheese

FOR THE BROCCOLI

- 4 cups broccoli florets
- 2 tablespoons olive oil, divided
- ¼ teaspoon kosher salt
- ¼ teaspoon freshly ground black pepper
- 2 teaspoons fresh lemon juice
- 2 tablespoons grated Parmesan cheese

1. **To prep the chicken Parmesan:** Set up a breading station with 3 small shallow bowls. Place the flour in the first bowl. In the second bowl, beat the eggs. Combine the panko, Parmesan, and Italian seasoning in the third bowl.

2. Bread the chicken cutlets in this order: First, dip them into the flour, coating both sides. Then, dip into the beaten egg. Finally, place in the panko mixture, coating both sides of the cutlets. Drizzle the oil over the cutlets.

CONTINUED >

Super swap: Pair this chicken Parmesan with Toasty Garlic Bread (page 54), Broiled Utica Greens (page 87), or Garlicky Roasted Broccoli (page 108).

3. To prep the broccoli: In a large bowl, combine the broccoli, 1 tablespoon of olive oil, the salt, and black pepper.

4. To cook the chicken and broccoli: Install a crisper plate in the Zone 1 basket. Place the chicken in the basket and insert the basket in the unit. Place the broccoli in the Zone 2 basket and insert the basket in the unit.

5. Select Zone 1, select AIR FRY, set the temperature to 390°F, and set the time to 18 minutes.

6. Select Zone 2, select ROAST, set the temperature to 390°F, and set the time to 15 minutes. Select SMART FINISH.™

7. Press START/PAUSE to begin cooking.

8. When the Zone 1 timer reads 10 minutes, press START/PAUSE. Remove the basket and use silicone-tipped tongs to flip the chicken. Reinsert the basket and press START/PAUSE to resume cooking.

9. When the Zone 1 timer reads 2 minutes, press START/PAUSE. Remove the basket and spoon 2 tablespoons of marinara sauce over each chicken cutlet. Sprinkle the mozzarella on top. Reinsert the basket and press START/PAUSE to resume cooking.

10. When cooking is complete, the cheese will be melted and the chicken cooked through (an instant-read thermometer should read 165°F). Transfer the broccoli to a large bowl. Add the lemon juice and Parmesan and toss to coat. Serve the chicken and broccoli warm.

Per serving: *Calories: 462; Total fat: 22g; Saturated fat: 5g; Carbohydrates: 25g; Fiber: 2.5g; Protein: 37g; Sodium: 838mg*

Coconut Chicken Tenders with Broiled Utica Greens

SERVES 4

Utica greens are traditionally made with sautéed greens and hot cherry peppers and topped with a crispy bread crumb and cheese topping. To adapt this regional favorite for the Ninja® Foodi® 2-Basket Air Fryer, I used frozen greens, which don't need to be cooked before broiling. Escarole is traditional, but you can substitute Swiss chard if it's easier to find. Utica greens are typically served as an appetizer, but I love the way the spicy peppers pair with sweet coconut chicken tenders.

NUT-FREE

Prep time: 10 minutes
Cook time: 25 minutes

FOR THE CHICKEN TENDERS

2 tablespoons
  all-purpose flour

2 large eggs

1 cup unsweetened
  shredded coconut

¾ cup panko bread crumbs

½ teaspoon kosher salt

1½ pounds chicken tenders

Nonstick cooking spray

FOR THE UTICA GREENS

12 ounces frozen chopped
  escarole or Swiss chard,
  thawed and drained

¼ cup diced prosciutto

2 tablespoons chopped
  pickled cherry peppers

½ teaspoon garlic powder

½ teaspoon onion powder

¼ teaspoon kosher salt

¼ cup Italian-style
  bread crumbs

¼ cup grated
  Romano cheese

Nonstick cooking spray

1. **To prep the chicken tenders:** Set up a breading station with three small shallow bowls. Place the flour in the first bowl. In the second bowl, beat the eggs. Combine the coconut, bread crumbs, and salt in the third bowl.

2. Bread the chicken tenders in this order: First, coat them in the flour. Then, dip into the beaten egg. Finally, coat them in the coconut breading, gently pressing the breading into the chicken to help it adhere. Mist both sides of each tender with cooking spray.

CONTINUED >

Super swap: Try these coconut chicken tenders with Street Corn (page 76), Seasoned Potato Wedges (page 155), or Pineapple Cauliflower Rice (page 78).

3. To prep the Utica greens: In the Zone 2 basket, mix the greens, prosciutto, cherry peppers, garlic powder, onion powder, and salt. Scatter the bread crumbs and Romano cheese over the top. Spritz the greens with cooking spray.

4. To cook the chicken and greens: Install a crisper plate in the Zone 1 basket. Place the chicken tenders in the basket in a single layer and insert the basket in the unit. Insert the Zone 2 basket in the unit.

5. Select Zone 1, select AIR FRY, set the temperature to 390°F, and set the time to 25 minutes.

6. Select Zone 2, select AIR BROIL, set the temperature to 450°F, and set the time to 10 minutes. Select SMART FINISH.™

7. Press START/PAUSE to begin cooking.

8. When cooking is complete, the chicken will be crispy and cooked through (an instant-read thermometer should read 165°F) and the greens should be warmed through and toasted on top. Serve warm.

Per serving: *Calories: 527; Total fat: 26g; Saturated fat: 11g; Carbohydrates: 24g; Fiber: 6.5g; Protein: 50g; Sodium: 886mg*

Roasted Garlic Chicken Pizza with Cauliflower "Wings"

SERVES 4

Pizza is one of my go-to dinners. I love this roasted garlic chicken version topped super gooey mozzarella cheese. Roast cauliflower tossed in Buffalo wing sauce is a fun alternative to traditional chicken wings and a great way to sneak in a serving of veggies!

NUT-FREE

Prep time: 10 minutes
Cook time: 25 minutes

FOR THE PIZZA

2 prebaked rectangular pizza crusts or flatbreads

2 tablespoons olive oil

1 tablespoon minced garlic

1½ cups shredded part-skim mozzarella cheese

6 ounces boneless, skinless chicken breast, thinly sliced

¼ teaspoon red pepper flakes (optional)

FOR THE CAULIFLOWER "WINGS"

4 cups cauliflower florets

1 tablespoon vegetable oil

½ cup Buffalo wing sauce

1. **To prep the pizza:** Trim the pizza crusts to fit in the air fryer basket, if necessary.

2. Brush the top of each crust with the oil and sprinkle with the garlic. Top the crusts with the mozzarella, chicken, and red pepper flakes (if using).

3. **To prep the cauliflower "wings":** In a large bowl, combine the cauliflower and oil and toss to coat the florets.

4. **To cook the pizza and "wings":** Install a crisper plate in each of the two baskets. Place one pizza in the Zone 1 basket and insert the basket in the unit. Place the cauliflower in the Zone 2 basket and insert the basket in the unit.

5. Select Zone 1, select ROAST, set the temperature to 375°F, and set the time to 25 minutes.

CONTINUED >

Variation: For a vegetarian version of this pizza, swap the chicken for thinly sliced eggplant or zucchini. It's also delicious with sliced roasted red peppers.

Super swap: This pizza also goes great with Buffalo Wings // Honey-Garlic Wings (page 56) or Spinach-Artichoke Stuffed Mushrooms (page 123).

6. Select Zone 2, select AIR FRY, set the temperature to 390°F, and set the time to 25 minutes. Select SMART FINISH.™

7. Press START/PAUSE to begin cooking.

8. When the Zone 1 timer reads 13 minutes, press START/PAUSE. Remove the basket. Transfer the pizza to a cutting board (the chicken should be cooked through and the cheese melted and bubbling). Add the second pizza to the basket. Reinsert the basket in the unit and press START/PAUSE to resume cooking.

9. When the Zone 2 timer reads 5 minutes, press START/PAUSE. Remove the basket and add the Buffalo wing sauce to the cauliflower. Shake well to evenly coat the cauliflower in the sauce. Reinsert the basket and press START/PAUSE to resume cooking.

10. When cooking is complete, the cauliflower will be crisp on the outside and tender inside, and the chicken on the second pizza will be cooked through and the cheese melted.

11. Cut each pizza into 4 slices. Serve with the cauliflower "wings" on the side.

Per serving: *Calories: 360; Total fat: 20g; Saturated fat: 6.5g; Carbohydrates: 21g; Fiber: 2.5g; Protein: 24g; Sodium: 1,399mg*

Spicy Chicken Sandwiches with "Fried" Pickles

SERVES 4

The secret to these fast food–style spicy chicken sandwiches is the few splashes of hot sauce in the breading. This adds flavor and just enough kick to keep things interesting without being too hot. If you like more heat, add cayenne pepper to the bread crumb mixture. Serve these sandwiches with your favorite sandwich toppings (pickle slices, lettuce, and mayonnaise are classic) and a side of crispy "fried" pickles.

DAIRY-FREE, NUT-FREE

Prep time: 15 minutes
Cook time: 18 minutes

FOR THE CHICKEN SANDWICHES

- 2 tablespoons all-purpose flour
- 2 large eggs
- 2 teaspoons Louisiana-style hot sauce
- 1 cup panko bread crumbs
- 1 teaspoon paprika
- ½ teaspoon garlic powder
- ¼ teaspoon salt
- ¼ teaspoon freshly ground black pepper
- ¼ teaspoon cayenne pepper (optional)
- 4 thin-sliced chicken cutlets (4 ounces each)
- 2 teaspoons vegetable oil
- 4 hamburger rolls

FOR THE PICKLES

- 1 cup dill pickle chips, drained
- 1 large egg
- ½ cup panko bread crumbs
- Nonstick cooking spray
- ½ cup ranch dressing, for serving (optional)

1. **To prep the sandwiches:** Set up a breading station with three small shallow bowls. Place the flour in the first bowl. In the second bowl, whisk together the eggs and hot sauce. Combine the panko, paprika, garlic powder, salt, black pepper, and cayenne pepper (if using) in the third bowl.

2. Bread the chicken cutlets in this order: First, dip them into the flour, coating both sides. Then, dip into the egg mixture. Finally, coat them in the panko mixture, gently pressing the breading into the chicken to help it adhere. Drizzle the cutlets with the oil. CONTINUED >

Super swap: These chicken sandwiches also go great with Sweet Potato Fries (page 157) or Barbecue Potato Chips (page 114).

3. **To prep the pickles:** Pat the pickles dry with a paper towel.

4. In a small shallow bowl, whisk the egg. Add the panko to a second shallow bowl.

5. Dip the pickles in the egg, then the panko. Mist both sides of the pickles with cooking spray.

6. **To cook the chicken and pickles:** Install a crisper plate in each of the two baskets. Place the chicken in the Zone 1 basket and insert the basket in the unit. Place the pickles in the Zone 2 basket and insert the basket in the unit.

7. Select Zone 1, select AIR FRY, set the temperature to 390°F, and set the time to 18 minutes.

8. Select Zone 2, select AIR FRY, set the temperature to 400°F, and set the time to 15 minutes. Select SMART FINISH.™

9. Press START/PAUSE to begin cooking.

10. When both timers read 10 minutes, press START/PAUSE. Remove the Zone 1 basket and use silicone-tipped tongs to flip the chicken. Reinsert the basket. Remove the Zone 2 basket and shake to redistribute the pickles. Reinsert the basket and press START/PAUSE to resume cooking.

11. When cooking is complete, the breading will be crisp and golden brown and the chicken cooked through (an instant-read thermometer should read 165°F). Place one chicken cutlet on each hamburger roll. Serve the "fried" pickles on the side with ranch dressing, if desired.

Per serving: Calories: 418; Total fat: 12g; Saturated fat: 1.5g; Carbohydrates: 42g; Fiber: 2g; Protein: 36g; Sodium: 839mg

"Fried" Chicken with Warm Baked Potato Salad

SERVES 4

Traditional fried chicken is delicious, but it's time-consuming to make and it can be difficult to keep the fry oil at a steady temperature. With the Ninja® Foodi® Air Fryer, the chicken comes out crispy and delicious with much less effort. The potato salad is a great side dish inspired by the flavors of a loaded baked potato. The potatoes will be very hot when they come out of the unit, so run them under cold water for a minute to cool them down. This salad should be served warm, but not steaming hot.

NUT-FREE

Prep time: 10 minutes, plus 40 minutes to rest
Cook time: 40 minutes

FOR THE "FRIED" CHICKEN

1 cup buttermilk

1 tablespoon kosher salt

4 bone-in, skin-on chicken drumsticks and/or thighs

2 cups all-purpose flour

1 tablespoon seasoned salt

1 tablespoon paprika

Nonstick cooking spray

FOR THE POTATO SALAD

1½ pounds baby red potatoes, halved

1 tablespoon vegetable oil

½ cup mayonnaise

⅓ cup plain reduced-fat Greek yogurt

1 tablespoon apple cider vinegar

½ teaspoon kosher salt

½ teaspoon freshly ground black pepper

¾ cup shredded Cheddar cheese

4 slices cooked bacon, crumbled

3 scallions, sliced

1. **To prep the chicken:** In a large bowl, combine the buttermilk and salt. Add the chicken and turn to coat. Let rest for at least 30 minutes (for the best flavor, marinate the chicken overnight in the refrigerator).

2. In a separate large bowl, combine the flour, seasoned salt, and paprika.

CONTINUED >

Super swap: You'll also enjoy this "fried" chicken with Street Corn (page 76) or Seasoned Potato Wedges (page 155).

3. Remove the chicken from the marinade and allow any excess marinade to drip off. Discard the marinade. Dip the chicken pieces in the flour, coating them thoroughly. Mist with cooking spray. Let the chicken rest for 10 minutes.

4. To prep the potatoes: In a large bowl, combine the potatoes and oil and toss to coat.

5. To cook the chicken and potatoes: Install a crisper plate in the Zone 1 basket. Place the chicken in the basket in a single layer and insert the basket in the unit. Place the potatoes in the Zone 2 basket and insert the basket in the unit.

6. Select Zone 1, select AIR FRY, set the temperature to 390°F, and set the time to 30 minutes.

7. Select Zone 2, select BAKE, set the temperature to 400°F, and set the time to 40 minutes. Select SMART FINISH.™

8. Press START/PAUSE to begin cooking.

9. When cooking is complete, the chicken will be golden brown and cooked through (an instant-read thermometer should read 165°F) and the potatoes will be fork-tender.

10. Rinse the potatoes under cold water for about 1 minute to cool them.

11. Place the potatoes in a large bowl and stir in the mayonnaise, yogurt, vinegar, salt, and black pepper. Gently stir in the Cheddar, bacon, and scallions. Serve warm with the "fried" chicken.

Per serving: *Calories: 639; Total fat: 38g; Saturated fat: 9.5g; Carbohydrates: 54g; Fiber: 4g; Protein: 21g; Sodium: 1,471mg*

Air-Fried Turkey Breast with Roasted Green Bean Casserole

SERVES 4

My take on a traditional holiday meal, this dish contains everything you love about Thanksgiving dinner but in a scaled-down size. Split turkey breast is a great alternative to cooking a full turkey, taking just under an hour when prepared in the Foodi® Air Fryer. You'll love the crispy skin! Of course, Thanksgiving dinner isn't complete without green bean casserole. This version is made with roasted green beans and has an extra crispy topping.

NUT-FREE

Prep time: 10 minutes, plus 15 minutes to rest
Cook time: 50 minutes

FOR THE TURKEY BREAST

2 teaspoons unsalted butter, at room temperature

1 bone-in split turkey breast (3 pounds), thawed if frozen

1 teaspoon poultry seasoning

½ teaspoon kosher salt

⅓ teaspoon freshly ground black pepper

FOR THE GREEN BEAN CASSEROLE

1 (10.5-ounce) can condensed cream of mushroom soup

½ cup whole milk

1 cup store-bought crispy fried onions, divided

¼ teaspoon kosher salt

¼ teaspoon freshly ground black pepper

1 pound green beans, trimmed

¼ cup panko bread crumbs

Nonstick cooking spray

1. **To prep the turkey breast:** Spread the butter over the skin side of the turkey. Season with the poultry seasoning, salt, and black pepper.

2. **To prep the green bean casserole:** In a medium bowl, combine the soup, milk, ½ cup of crispy onions, the salt, and black pepper.

3. **To cook the turkey and beans:** Install a crisper plate in the Zone 1 basket. Place the turkey skin-side up in the basket and insert the basket in the unit. Place the green beans in the Zone 2 basket and insert the basket in the unit.

4. Select Zone 1, select AIR FRY, set the temperature to 360ºF, and set the time to 50 minutes.

5. Select Zone 2, select ROAST, set the temperature to 350ºF, and set the time to 40 minutes. Select SMART FINISH.™

6. Press START/PAUSE to begin cooking.

7. When the Zone 2 timer reads 30 minutes, press START/PAUSE. Remove the basket and stir the soup mixture into the beans. Scatter the panko and remaining ½ cup of crispy onions over the top, then spritz with cooking spray. Reinsert the basket and press START/PAUSE to resume cooking.

8. When cooking is complete, the turkey will be cooked through (an instant-read thermometer should read 165ºF) and the green bean casserole will be bubbling and golden brown on top.

9. Let the turkey and casserole rest for at least 15 minutes before serving.

Per serving: Calories: 577; Total fat: 22g; Saturated fat: 6.5g; Carbohydrates: 24g; Fiber: 3.5g; Protein: 68g; Sodium: 1,165mg

Super swap: Try this turkey breast with Apple and Sage Stuffing (page 101), Roasted Vegetable Salad (page 98), or Lemon-Feta Baby Potatoes (page 126).

Ranch Turkey Tenders with Roasted Vegetable Salad

SERVES 4

Ranch dressing gives these crispy turkey tenders a real flavor punch. The salad is a great way to use up any sturdy vegetables that you have in the fridge at the end of the week. I like serving the vegetables with balsamic vinaigrette for a bright, vibrant flavor, but you could use ranch dressing on the salad, too.

Prep time: 15 minutes
Cook time: 20 minutes

FOR THE TURKEY TENDERS

1 pound turkey tenderloin

¼ cup ranch dressing

½ cup panko bread crumbs

Nonstick cooking spray

FOR THE VEGETABLE SALAD

1 large sweet potato, peeled and diced

1 zucchini, diced

1 red bell pepper, diced

1 small red onion, sliced

1 tablespoon vegetable oil

¼ teaspoon kosher salt

½ teaspoon freshly ground black pepper

2 cups baby spinach

½ cup store-bought balsamic vinaigrette

¼ cup chopped walnuts

1. **To prep the turkey tenders:** Slice the turkey crosswise into 16 strips. Brush both sides of each strip with ranch dressing, then coat with the panko. Press the bread crumbs into the turkey to help them adhere. Mist both sides of the strips with cooking spray.

2. **To prep the vegetables:** In a large bowl, combine the sweet potato, zucchini, bell pepper, onion, and vegetable oil. Stir well to coat the vegetables. Season with the salt and black pepper.

3. **To cook the turkey and vegetables:** Install a crisper plate in the Zone 1 basket. Place the turkey tenders in the basket in a single layer and insert the basket in the unit. Place the vegetables in the Zone 2 basket and insert the basket in the unit.

4. Select Zone 1, select AIR FRY, set the temperature to 375°F, and set the time to 20 minutes.

5. Select Zone 2, select ROAST, set the temperature to 400°F, and set the time to 20 minutes. Select SMART FINISH.™

6. Press START/PAUSE to begin cooking.

7. When both timers read 10 minutes, press START/PAUSE. Remove the Zone 1 basket and use silicone tipped tongs to flip the turkey tenders. Reinsert the basket in the unit. Remove the Zone 2 basket and shake to redistribute the vegetables. Reinsert the basket and press START/PAUSE to resume cooking.

8. When cooking is complete, the turkey will be golden brown and cooked through (an instant-read thermometer should read 165°F) and the vegetables will be fork-tender.

9. Place the spinach in a large serving bowl. Mix in the roasted vegetables and balsamic vinaigrette. Sprinkle with walnuts. Serve warm with the turkey tenders.

Super swap: Pair these turkey tenders with Sweet Potato Fries (page 157) or Crispy Kale Chips (page 74).

Per serving: Calories: 470; Total fat: 28g; Saturated fat: 2.5g; Carbohydrates: 28g; Fiber: 4g; Protein: 31g; Sodium: 718mg

Maple-Mustard Glazed Turkey Tenderloin with Apple and Sage Stuffing

SERVES 4

Whether you call it stuffing or dressing, pretty much everyone can agree that this side dish is the best part of a turkey dinner. Apple and sage give this stuffing a fresh and autumnal feel, but it's so good you'll want to eat it year-round. Boneless turkey tenderloin cooks so much faster than a full turkey, so it's easy to make this meal whenever the mood strikes.

NUT-FREE

Prep time: 10 minutes
Cook time: 35 minutes

FOR THE TURKEY TENDERLOIN

2 tablespoons maple syrup

1 tablespoon unsalted butter, at room temperature

1 tablespoon Dijon mustard

½ teaspoon kosher salt

½ teaspoon freshly ground black pepper

1½ pounds turkey tenderloin

FOR THE STUFFING

6 ounces seasoned stuffing mix

1½ cups chicken broth

1 apple, peeled, cored, and diced

1 tablespoon chopped fresh sage

2 teaspoons unsalted butter, cut into several pieces

1. **To prep the turkey tenderloin:** In a small bowl, mix the maple syrup, butter, mustard, salt, and black pepper until smooth. Spread the maple mixture over the entire turkey tenderloin.

2. **To prep the stuffing:** In the Zone 2 basket, combine the stuffing mix and chicken broth. Stir well to ensure the bread is fully moistened. Stir in the apple and sage. Scatter the butter on top.

CONTINUED >

Super swap: Pair these turkey tenderloins with Roasted Green Bean Casserole (page 96), Garlicky Roasted Broccoli (page 108), or Baked Brown Sugar Acorn Squash (page 139).

3. To cook the turkey and stuffing: Install a crisper plate in the Zone 1 basket. Place the turkey tenderloin in the basket and insert the basket in the unit. Insert the Zone 2 basket in the unit.

4. Select Zone 1, select AIR FRY, set the temperature to 390°F, and set the time to 35 minutes.

5. Select Zone 2, select BAKE, set the temperature to 340°F, and set the time to 20 minutes. Select SMART FINISH.™

6. Press START/PAUSE to begin cooking.

7. When the Zone 2 timer reads 10 minutes, press START/PAUSE. Remove the basket and stir the stuffing. Reinsert the basket and press START/PAUSE to resume cooking.

8. When cooking is complete, the turkey will be cooked through (an instant-read thermometer should read 165°F) and the stuffing will have absorbed all the liquid and be slightly crisp on top. Serve warm.

Per serving: *Calories: 455; Total fat: 10g; Saturated fat: 3g; Carbohydrates: 42g; Fiber: 2.5g; Protein: 46g; Sodium: 1,230mg*

Turkey Meatloaf with Veggie Medley

SERVES 4

I love using my Ninja® Foodi® 2-Basket Air Fryer to cook classic comfort food. This turkey meatloaf is moist and flavorful, with the perfect ratio of bread crumbs to ground turkey. For the best texture, be sure to let the egg and bread crumb mixture sit for a few minutes before adding the ground turkey.

DAIRY-FREE, NUT-FREE

Prep time: 15 minutes
Cook time: 30 minutes

FOR THE MEATLOAF

1 large egg

¼ cup ketchup

2 teaspoons Worcestershire sauce

½ cup Italian-style bread crumbs

1 teaspoon kosher salt

1 pound ground turkey (93 percent lean)

1 tablespoon vegetable oil

FOR THE VEGGIE MEDLEY

2 carrots, thinly sliced

8 ounces green beans, trimmed (about 2 cups)

2 cups broccoli florets

1 red bell pepper, sliced into strips

2 tablespoons vegetable oil

½ teaspoon kosher salt

½ teaspoon freshly ground black pepper

1. **To prep the meatloaf:** In a large bowl, whisk the egg. Stir in the ketchup, Worcestershire sauce, bread crumbs, and salt. Let sit for 5 minutes to allow the bread crumbs to absorb some moisture.

2. Gently mix in the turkey until just incorporated. Form the mixture into a loaf. Brush with the oil.

3. **To prep the veggie medley:** In a large bowl, combine the carrots, green beans, broccoli, bell pepper, oil, salt, and black pepper. Mix well to coat the vegetables with the oil.

CONTINUED >

Turkey Meatloaf with Veggie Medley continued

Super swap: This meatloaf also pairs nicely with Roasted Vegetable Salad (page 98), Scalloped Potatoes and Cauliflower (page 131), or Baked Brown Sugar Acorn Squash (page 139).

4. To cook the meatloaf and veggie medley: Install a crisper plate in each of the two baskets. Place the meatloaf in the Zone 1 basket and insert the basket in the unit. Place the vegetables in the Zone 2 basket and insert the basket in the unit.

5. Select Zone 1, select ROAST, set the temperature to 350ºF, and set the time to 30 minutes.

6. Select Zone 2, select AIR FRY, set the temperature to 390ºF, and set the time to 20 minutes. Select SMART FINISH.™

7. Press START/PAUSE to begin cooking.

8. When cooking is complete, the meatloaf will be cooked through (an instant-read thermometer should read165ºF) and the vegetables will be tender and roasted.

Per serving: Calories: 394; Total fat: 20g; Saturated fat: 4.5g; Carbohydrates: 25g; Fiber: 4.5g; Protein: 28g; Sodium: 952mg

Cheeseburger with Barbecue Potato Chips, *page 114*

5

Beef, Pork, and Lamb

Italian-Style Meatballs with Garlicky Roasted Broccoli

SERVES 4

I absolutely adore meatballs and making them in the Ninja® Foodi® Air Fryer is so easy. I especially love that there's no need for frying oil and no big mess to clean up afterward. For something a little lighter than pasta, I like to serve them with my all-time favorite broccoli recipe. It's cooked to tender-crisp perfection and has tons of flavor from red pepper flakes and a generous helping of garlic that gets slightly toasted as the broccoli roasts.

NUT-FREE

Prep time: 20 minutes
Cook time: 15 minutes

FOR THE MEATBALLS
1 large egg

¼ cup Italian-style
   bread crumbs

1 pound ground beef
   (85 percent lean)

¼ cup grated
   Parmesan cheese

¼ teaspoon kosher salt

Nonstick cooking spray

2 cups marinara sauce

FOR THE ROASTED BROCCOLI
4 cups broccoli florets

1 tablespoon olive oil

¼ teaspoon kosher salt

¼ teaspoon freshly
   ground pepper

¼ teaspoon red
   pepper flakes

1 tablespoon minced garlic

1. **To prep the meatballs:** In a large bowl, beat the egg. Mix in the bread crumbs and let sit for 5 minutes.

2. Add the beef, Parmesan, and salt and mix until just combined. Form the meatball mixture into 8 meatballs, about 1 inch in diameter. Mist with cooking spray.

3. **To prep the broccoli:** In a large bowl, combine the broccoli, olive oil, salt, black pepper, and red pepper flakes. Toss to coat the broccoli evenly.

4. To cook the meatballs and broccoli: Install a crisper plate in the Zone 1 basket. Place the meatballs in the basket and insert the basket in the unit. Place the broccoli in the Zone 2 basket, sprinkle the garlic over the broccoli, and insert the basket in the unit.

5. Select Zone 1, select AIR FRY, set the temperature to 400°F, and set the time to 12 minutes.

6. Select Zone 2, select ROAST, set the temperature to 390°F, and set the time to 15 minutes. Select SMART FINISH.™

7. Press START/PAUSE to begin cooking.

8. When the Zone 1 timer reads 5 minutes, press START/PAUSE. Remove the basket and pour the marinara sauce over the meatballs. Reinsert the basket and press START/PAUSE to resume cooking.

9. When cooking is complete, the meatballs should be cooked through and the broccoli will have begun to brown on the edges.

Super swap: Pair these meatballs with Broiled Utica Greens (page 87) or Crispy Zucchini Noodles (page 187).

Per serving: Calories: 493; Total fat: 33g; Saturated fat: 9g; Carbohydrates: 24g; Fiber: 3g; Protein: 31g; Sodium: 926mg

Mongolian Beef with Sweet Chili Brussels Sprouts

Mongolian beef is typically prepared in a wok over extremely high heat to cara-melize the outside of the beef while keeping the meat nice and tender. The intense heat of the Foodi® Air Fryer results in a very similar texture. I paired this with sweet chili Brussels sprouts, inspired by one of my favorite local restaurants.

DAIRY-FREE, NUT-FREE

Prep time: 10 minutes
Cook time: 20 minutes

FOR THE MONGOLIAN BEEF

- 1 pound flank steak, cut into thin strips
- 1 tablespoon olive oil
- 2 tablespoons cornstarch
- ½ cup reduced-sodium soy sauce
- ½ cup packed light brown sugar
- 1 tablespoon chili paste (optional)
- 1 tablespoon minced garlic
- 1 tablespoon minced fresh ginger
- 2 scallions, chopped

FOR THE BRUSSELS SPROUTS

- 1 pound Brussels sprouts, halved lengthwise
- 1 tablespoon olive oil
- ½ cup gochujang sauce
- 2 tablespoons rice vinegar
- 1 tablespoon reduced-sodium soy sauce
- 1 tablespoon light brown sugar
- 1 teaspoon fresh garlic

1. **To prep the Mongolian beef:** In a large bowl, combine the flank steak and olive oil and toss to coat. Add the cornstarch and toss to coat.

2. In a small bowl, whisk together the soy sauce, brown sugar, chili paste (if using), garlic, and ginger. Set the soy sauce mixture aside.

3. **To prep the Brussels sprouts:** In a large bowl, combine the Brussels sprouts and oil and toss to coat.

4. In a small bowl, whisk together the gochujang sauce, vinegar, soy sauce, brown sugar, and garlic. Set the chili sauce mixture aside.

5. **To cook the beef and Brussels sprouts:** Install a crisper plate in each of the two baskets. Place the beef in the Zone 1 basket and insert the basket in the unit. Place the Brussels sprouts in the Zone 2 basket and insert the basket in the unit.

6. Select Zone 1, select AIR FRY, set the temperature to 390°F, and set the time to 15 minutes.

7. Select Zone 2, select AIR FRY, set the temperature to 400°F, and set the time to 20 minutes. Select SMART FINISH.™

8. Press START/PAUSE to begin cooking.

9. When both timers read 5 minutes, press START/PAUSE. Remove the Zone 1 basket, add the reserved soy sauce mixture and the scallions, and toss with the beef. Reinsert the basket. Remove the Zone 2 basket, add the reserved chili sauce mixture, and toss with the Brussels sprouts. Reinsert the basket and press START/PAUSE to resume cooking.

10. When cooking is complete, the steak should be cooked through and the Brussels sprouts tender and slightly caramelized. Serve warm.

Per serving: Calories: 481; Total fat: 16g; Saturated fat: 4.5g; Carbohydrates: 60g; Fiber: 5g; Protein: 27g; Sodium: 2,044mg

Super swap: Try this Mongolian beef with Roasted Snap Peas and Scallions (page 80) or Seasoned Rice (page 29).

Balsamic Steak Tips with Roasted Asparagus and Mushroom Medley

SERVES 4

Fork-tender steak tips are the perfect addition to any dinner, and I love how this balsamic marinade highlights their beefy flavor. I paired the steak with roasted veggies and a mushroom medley for a super-savory dinner.

DAIRY-FREE, NUT-FREE

Prep time: 10 minutes
Cook time: 25 minutes

FOR THE STEAK TIPS
1½ pounds sirloin tips

½ cup olive oil

¼ cup balsamic vinegar

¼ cup packed light
   brown sugar

1 tablespoon
   reduced-sodium
   soy sauce

1 teaspoon finely chopped
   fresh rosemary

1 teaspoon minced garlic

FOR THE ASPARAGUS AND MUSHROOMS
6 ounces sliced cremini
   mushrooms

1 small red onion, sliced

1 tablespoon olive oil

1 pound asparagus,
   tough ends trimmed

⅛ teaspoon kosher salt

1. **To prep the steak tips:** In a large bowl, combine the sirloin tips, oil, vinegar, brown sugar, soy sauce, rosemary, and garlic. Mix well to coat the steak.

2. **To prep the mushrooms:** In a large bowl, combine the mushrooms, onion, and oil.

3. **To cook the steak and vegetables:** Install a crisper plate in each of the two baskets. Shake any excess marinade from the steak tips, place the steak in the Zone 1 basket, and insert the basket in the unit. Place the mushrooms and onions in the Zone 2 basket and insert the basket in the unit.

4. Select Zone 1, select AIR FRY, set the temperature to 400°F, and set the time to 12 minutes.

5. Select Zone 2, select ROAST, set the temperature to 400°F, and set the time to 25 minutes. Select SMART FINISH.™

6. Press START/PAUSE to begin cooking.

7. When the Zone 2 timer reads 10 minutes, press START/PAUSE. Remove the basket, add the asparagus to the mushrooms and onion, and sprinkle with salt. Reinsert the basket and press START/PAUSE to resume cooking.

8. When cooking is complete, the beef should be cooked to your liking and the asparagus crisp-tender. Serve warm.

Per serving: Calories: 524; Total fat: 33g; Saturated fat: 2.5g; Carbohydrates: 16g; Fiber: 3g; Protein: 41g; Sodium: 192mg

Super swap: Enjoy these steak tips with Buttery Roasted Radishes (page 72), Hasselback Potatoes (page 119), or Peppers, Potatoes, and Onions (page 137).

Cheeseburgers with Barbecue Potato Chips

SERVES 4

Enjoy the classic flavors of a summer cookout year-round! These burgers are so juicy and flavorful that I actually prefer them to grilled burgers. The burgers in this recipe are cooked to medium, so adjust the timing up or down by a minute or two to your preference. You'll love the way the burgers pair with homemade barbecue potato chips. For maximum crispiness, be sure to slice the potatoes paper thin—if you have a mandoline slicer, now is the time to pull it out—and shake the basket frequently while they fry.

NUT-FREE

Prep time: 15 minutes, plus 30 minutes to soak
Cook time: 15 minutes

FOR THE CHEESEBURGERS

1 pound ground beef (85 percent lean)

¼ teaspoon kosher salt

¼ teaspoon freshly ground black pepper

½ teaspoon olive oil

4 slices American cheese

4 hamburger rolls

FOR THE POTATO CHIPS

2 large russet potatoes

2 teaspoons vegetable oil

1½ teaspoons smoked paprika

1 teaspoon light brown sugar

½ teaspoon garlic powder

½ teaspoon kosher salt

¼ teaspoon chili powder

1. **To prep the cheeseburgers:** Season the beef with the salt and black pepper. Form the beef into 4 patties about 1 inch thick. Brush both sides of the beef patties with the oil.

2. **To prep the potato chips:** Fill a large bowl with ice water. Using a mandoline or sharp knife, cut the potatoes into very thin (⅛- to 1/16-inch) slices. Soak the potatoes in the ice water for 30 minutes.

3. Drain the potatoes and pat dry with a paper towel. Place in a large bowl and toss with the oil, smoked paprika, brown sugar, garlic powder, salt, and chili powder.

4. To cook the cheeseburgers and potato chips:
Install a crisper plate in each of the two baskets. Place the burgers in the Zone 1 basket and insert the basket in the unit. Place the potato slices in the Zone 2 basket and insert the basket in the unit.

5. Select Zone 1, select AIR FRY, set the temperature to 390°F, and set the time to 12 minutes.

6. Select Zone 2, select AIR FRY, set the temperature to 390°F, and set the time to 15 minutes. Select SMART FINISH.™

7. Press START/PAUSE to begin cooking.

8. At 5-minute intervals, press START/PAUSE. Remove the Zone 2 basket and shake the potato chips to keep them from sticking to each other. Reinsert the basket and press START/PAUSE to resume cooking.

9. When cooking is complete, the burgers should be cooked to your preferred doneness and the potato chips should be crisp and golden brown.

10. Top each burger patty in the basket with a slice of cheese. Turn the air fryer off and let the cheese melt inside the unit, or cover the basket with aluminum foil and let stand for 1 to 2 minutes, until the cheese is melted. Serve the cheeseburgers on buns with the chips on the side.

Per serving: Calories: 475; Total fat: 22g; Saturated fat: 8g; Carbohydrates: 38g; Fiber: 2g; Protein: 32g; Sodium: 733mg

Super swap: Try these cheeseburgers with Street Corn (page 76), "Fried" Okra (page 150), or Zucchini Chips (page 184).

Beef and Bean Taquitos with Mexican Rice

SERVES 4

The ingredients for these crispy air-fried taquitos are so simple, but they're jam-packed with flavor and taste just like the ones from my favorite local restaurant. Since ground beef puffs up when it cooks, it can bust through the tortillas if you add the filling while it's still raw. I solved this problem by partially cooking the beef right in the air fryer before combining it with the beans and rolling up the taquitos.

NUT-FREE

Prep time: 15 minutes
Cook time: 15 minutes

FOR THE TAQUITOS

½ **pound ground beef (85 percent lean)**

1 **tablespoon taco seasoning**

8 **(6-inch) soft white corn tortillas**

Nonstick cooking spray

¾ **cup canned refried beans**

½ **cup shredded Mexican blend cheese (optional)**

FOR THE MEXICAN RICE

1 **cup dried instant white rice (not microwavable)**

1½ **cups chicken broth**

¼ **cup jarred salsa**

2 **tablespoons canned tomato sauce**

1 **tablespoon vegetable oil**

½ **teaspoon kosher salt**

1. **To prep the taquitos:** In a large bowl, mix the ground beef and taco seasoning until well combined.

2. Mist both sides of each tortilla lightly with cooking spray.

3. **To prep the Mexican rice:** In the Zone 2 basket, combine the rice, broth, salsa, tomato sauce, oil, and salt. Stir well to ensure all of the rice is submerged in the liquid.

4. **To cook the taquitos and rice:** Install a crisper plate in the Zone 1 basket. Place the seasoned beef in the basket and insert the basket in the unit. Insert the Zone 2 basket in the unit.

5. Select Zone 1, select AIR FRY, set the temperature to 390ºF, and set the time to 15 minutes.

6. Select Zone 2, select BAKE, set the temperature to 350ºF, and set the time to 10 minutes. Select SMART FINISH.™

7. Press START/PAUSE to begin cooking.

8. When the Zone 1 timer reads 10 minutes, press START/PAUSE. Remove the basket and transfer the beef to a medium bowl. Add the refried beans and cheese (if using) and combine well. Spoon 2 tablespoons of the filling onto each tortilla and roll tightly. Place the taquitos in the Zone 1 basket seam-side down. Reinsert the basket in the unit and press START/PAUSE to resume cooking.

9. When cooking is complete, the taquitos should be crisp and golden brown and the rice cooked through. Serve hot.

Per serving: Calories: 431; Total fat: 18g; Saturated fat: 4g; Carbohydrates: 52g; Fiber: 5.5g; Protein: 18g; Sodium: 923mg

Prep tip: Store-bought salsa is a great shortcut ingredient that adds the flavor of tomato, onion, peppers, and seasonings all in one step.

Super swap: Try these taquitos with Street Corn (page 76) or Buttery Roasted Radishes (page 72).

Strip Steaks with Hasselback Potatoes

SERVES 4

I used to always cook my steaks in a cast-iron pan, but I hated having to babysit the pan and watch for flare-ups. Making them in an air fryer is so much easier. They get that same gorgeous crust, but the inside cooks perfectly with less guessing as to when they are done. Use the second basket to bake crispy Hasselback potatoes (also known as accordion potatoes). The garlic and herb butter seeps into the cracks, giving them so much flavor.

GLUTEN-FREE, NUT-FREE

Prep time: 15 minutes, plus 5 minutes to rest
Cook time: 30 minutes

FOR THE STRIP STEAK

2 boneless strip steaks (8 ounces each)

2 teaspoons vegetable oil

1 tablespoon steak seasoning

FOR THE HASSELBACK POTATOES

4 russet potatoes

1 tablespoon vegetable oil

1 teaspoon kosher salt

1 tablespoon salted butter, at room temperature

2 teaspoons minced garlic

2 teaspoons minced fresh parsley

1. **To prep the strip steak:** Brush both sides of the steaks with the oil and season with the steak seasoning.

2. **To prep the Hasselback potatoes:** Set a potato on a work surface and lay the handles of two wooden spoons lengthwise on either side of the potato. Make crosswise slits along the potato, spacing them ⅛ inch apart, being careful to not cut the potato completely through (the spoon handles will prevent you from cutting all the way through). Repeat with the remaining potatoes.

3. Rub the potatoes with the oil and season with salt.

4. In a small bowl, mix the butter, garlic, and parsley until smooth.

CONTINUED >

Strip Steaks with Hasselback Potatoes continued

Super swap: These strip steaks also go great with Broiled Utica Greens (page 87), Spinach-Artichoke Stuffed Mushrooms (page 123), or Scalloped Potatoes and Cauliflower (page 131).

5. To cook the steak and potatoes: Install a crisper plate in each of the two baskets. Place the steaks in the Zone 1 basket and insert the basket in the unit. Place the potatoes in the Zone 2 basket and insert the basket in the unit.

6. Select Zone 1, select AIR FRY, set the temperature to 375°F, and set the time to 20 minutes.

7. Select Zone 2, select BAKE, set the temperature to 375°F, and set the time to 30 minutes. Select SMART FINISH.™

8. Press START/PAUSE to begin cooking.

9. When both timers read 6 minutes, press START/PAUSE. Remove the Zone 1 basket and use silicone-tipped tongs to flip the steaks. Reinsert the basket in the unit. Remove the Zone 2 basket and spread the herb butter into the potatoes, being sure to work the butter in between the slices. Reinsert the basket and press START/PAUSE to resume cooking.

10. When cooking is complete, the steak should be cooked to your liking and the potato soft when pierced with a fork.

11. Remove the steaks from the basket and let rest for 5 minutes before slicing.

Per serving: Calories: 361; Total fat: 15g; Saturated fat: 5g; Carbohydrates: 31g; Fiber: 2g; Protein: 25g; Sodium: 694mg

Roast Beef with Yorkshire Pudding

SERVES 6

This impressive main course is perfect for dinner parties, especially during the holidays! I love making this roast beef in my Ninja® Foodi® 2-Basket Air Fryer because it cooks so quickly and comes out really tender. Serve this roast with Yorkshire pudding, a classic British side dish that's similar to a savory popover or soufflé, to soak up all of the delicious beef juices. Since we're making one big pudding instead of individual portions, it will be a little flatter in the center than is traditional, but it's still super delicious.

NUT-FREE

Prep time: 10 minutes, plus 15 minutes to rest
Cook time: 40 minutes

FOR THE ROAST BEEF
- **3-pound beef roast, trimmed**
- **1 tablespoon vegetable oil**
- **½ teaspoon kosher salt**
- **½ teaspoon freshly ground black pepper**
- **½ teaspoon garlic powder**
- **½ teaspoon onion powder**
- **½ teaspoon dried thyme**

FOR THE YORKSHIRE PUDDING
- **3 large eggs**
- **¾ cup whole milk**
- **2 tablespoons beef broth**
- **¾ cup all-purpose flour**
- **½ teaspoon kosher salt**
- **2 teaspoons unsalted butter**

1. **To prep the roast beef:** If necessary, trim the beef roast to fit in the Zone 1 basket. Rub the beef with the oil.

2. In a small bowl, combine the salt, black pepper, garlic powder, onion powder, and thyme. Rub the spice mixture all over the beef roast.

3. **To prep the Yorkshire pudding:** In a large bowl, whisk the eggs, milk, and beef broth until well combined. Whisk in the flour and salt to form a thin batter.

4. **To cook the beef and Yorkshire pudding:** Install a crisper plate in the Zone 1 basket. Place the beef roast in the basket and insert the basket in the unit. Place the butter in the Zone 2 basket and insert the basket in the unit.

CONTINUED >

Super swap: Pair this roast beef with Brown Sugar–Pecan Sweet Potatoes (page 133), Scalloped Potatoes and Cauliflower (page 131), or Roasted Green Bean Casserole (page 96).

5. Select Zone 1, select AIR FRY, set the temperature to 375ºF, and set the time to 40 minutes for a medium-rare roast (set to 50 minutes for medium or 60 minutes for well done).

6. Select Zone 2, select BAKE, set the temperature to 400ºF, and set the time to 20 minutes. Select SMART FINISH.™

7. Press START/PAUSE to begin cooking.

8. When the Zone 2 timer reads 18 minutes, press START/PAUSE. Remove the basket and pour the batter into it. Reinsert the basket and press START/PAUSE to resume cooking.

9. When cooking is complete, the beef should be cooked to your liking and the Yorkshire pudding should be fluffy on the edges and set in the center.

10. Remove the beef from the basket and let rest for at least 15 minutes before slicing.

11. Cut the Yorkshire pudding into 6 servings and serve the sliced beef on top.

Per serving: Calories: 517; Total fat: 26g; Saturated fat: 9.5g; Carbohydrates: 13g; Fiber: 0.5g; Protein: 52g; Sodium: 354mg

Pigs in a Blanket with Spinach-Artichoke Stuffed Mushrooms

SERVES 4

I don't know anyone who doesn't love pigs in a blanket. They're just so fun! And they're super fast to make in the Foodi® Air Fryer. Here I've paired them with stuffed mushrooms to keep the party vibe going. Freeze the leftover crescent roll dough for next time.

NUT-FREE

Prep time: 10 minutes
Cook time: 15 minutes

FOR THE PIGS IN A BLANKET

Half an 8-ounce tube refrigerated crescent roll dough

4 hot dogs

½ teaspoon everything bagel seasoning (optional)

FOR THE STUFFED MUSHROOMS

1 cup frozen chopped spinach, thawed and drained

1 (14-ounce) can artichoke hearts, drained and chopped

2 ounces (¼ cup) cream cheese, at room temperature

¼ cup grated Parmesan cheese

½ teaspoon garlic powder

1 (8-ounce) package whole cremini mushrooms, stems removed

1. **To prep the pigs in a blanket:** Unroll the crescent roll dough. It will be scored into 4 triangular pieces, but leave them in place and pinch together at the seams to form 1 large square of dough. Cut the dough into 4 strips.

2. Wrap one strip of dough around each hot dog, starting with a short end of the strips and wrapping in a spiral motion around the hot dog. If desired, sprinkle each pig in a blanket with everything bagel seasoning.

3. **To prep the stuffed mushrooms:** In a medium bowl, combine the spinach, artichoke hearts, cream cheese, Parmesan, and garlic powder. Stuff about 1 tablespoon of filling into each mushroom cap.

CONTINUED >

Pigs in a Blanket with Spinach-Artichoke Stuffed Mushrooms continued

Super swap: Try the pigs in a blanket with Baked Macaroni and Cheese (page 148), Seasoned Potato Wedges (page 155), or Crispy Kale Chips (page 74).

4. To cook the pigs in a blanket and mushrooms: Install a crisper plate in each of the two baskets. Place the pigs in a blanket in the Zone 1 basket and insert the basket in the unit. Place the mushrooms in the Zone 2 basket and insert the basket in the unit.

5. Select Zone 1, select AIR FRY, set the temperature to 370°F, and set the time to 8 minutes.

6. Select Zone 2, select BAKE, set the temperature to 370°F, and set the time to 15 minutes. Select SMART FINISH.™

7. Press START/PAUSE to begin cooking.

8. When cooking is complete, the crescent roll dough should be cooked through and golden brown, and the mushrooms should be tender.

Per serving: *Calories: 371; Total fat: 25g; Saturated fat: 11g; Carbohydrates: 22g; Fiber: 2.5g; Protein: 14g; Sodium: 1,059mg*

Roast Souvlaki-Style Pork with Lemon-Feta Baby Potatoes

SERVES 4

Souvlaki is a traditional Greek dish made from marinated and skewered meat that is grilled, similar to a kebab. For this recipe, I used a traditional souvlaki-style marinade but eliminated the process of threading the meat onto skewers. I designed this as a quick recipe, but for more flavor or if you want to get a jump start on preparing dinner, you can marinate the pork in the refrigerator up to 24 hours ahead.

GLUTEN-FREE, NUT-FREE

Prep time: 10 minutes
Cook time: 40 minutes

FOR THE PORK

1½ pounds pork tenderloin, cut into bite-size cubes

¼ cup olive oil

¼ cup fresh lemon juice

2 teaspoons minced garlic

2 teaspoons honey

1½ teaspoons dried oregano

¼ teaspoon kosher salt

¼ teaspoon freshly ground black pepper

FOR THE POTATOES

1 pound baby red or yellow potatoes, halved

1 tablespoon olive oil

Grated zest and juice of 1 lemon

½ teaspoon kosher salt

¼ teaspoon freshly ground black pepper

⅓ cup crumbled feta cheese

2 tablespoons chopped fresh parsley

1. **To prep the pork:** In a large bowl, combine the pork, oil, lemon juice, garlic, honey, oregano, salt, and black pepper. If desired, cover and refrigerate up to 24 hours.

2. **To prep the potatoes:** In a large bowl, combine the potatoes, oil, lemon zest, lemon juice, salt, and black pepper. Mix to coat the potatoes.

3. **To cook the pork and potatoes:** Install a crisper plate in each of the two baskets. Place the pork in the Zone 1 basket and insert the basket in the unit. Place the potatoes in the Zone 2 basket and insert the basket in the unit.

4. Select Zone 1, select ROAST, set the temperature to 390ºF, and set the time to 20 minutes.

5. Select Zone 2, select AIR FRY, set the temperature to 400ºF, and set the time to 40 minutes. Select SMART FINISH.™

6. Press START/PAUSE to begin cooking.

7. When cooking is complete, the pork will be cooked through (an instant-read thermometer should read 145ºF) and the potatoes will be tender and beginning to brown around the edges.

8. Stir the feta and parsley into the potatoes. Serve the pork and potatoes while hot.

Per serving: *Calories: 395; Total fat: 17g; Saturated fat: 4.5g; Carbohydrates: 24g; Fiber: 2g; Protein: 37g; Sodium: 399mg*

Super swap: Try this delicious pork with Peppers, Potatoes, and Onions (page 137) or Garlicky Roasted Broccoli (page 108).

Pork Katsu with Seasoned Rice

SERVES 4

This dish is my take on the popular Japanese-style breaded and fried pork cutlets with sweet barbecue sauce. I use panko bread crumbs for the coating because they are extra crispy when cooked in an air fryer. Toasted sesame seeds and scallions dress up the simple steamed rice served on the side.

DAIRY-FREE, NUT-FREE

Prep time: 15 minutes
Cook time: 15 minutes

FOR THE PORK KATSU

4 thin-sliced boneless pork chops (4 ounces each)

2 tablespoons all-purpose flour

2 large eggs

1 cup panko bread crumbs

¼ teaspoon kosher salt

¼ teaspoon freshly ground black pepper

1 teaspoon vegetable oil

3 tablespoons ketchup

3 tablespoons Worcestershire sauce

1 tablespoon oyster sauce

⅛ teaspoon granulated sugar

FOR THE RICE

2 cups dried instant rice (not microwavable)

2½ cups water

1 tablespoon sesame oil

1 teaspoon soy sauce

1 tablespoon toasted sesame seeds

3 scallions, sliced

1. To prep the pork katsu: Place the pork chops between two slices of plastic wrap. Using a meat mallet or rolling pin, pound the pork into ½-inch-thick cutlets.

2. Set up a breading station with three small shallow bowls. Place the flour in the first bowl. In the second bowl, whisk the eggs. Combine the panko, salt, and black pepper in the third bowl.

3. Bread the cutlets in this order: First, dip them in the flour, coating both sides. Then, dip them into the beaten egg. Finally, coat them in panko, gently pressing the bread crumbs to adhere to the pork. Drizzle both sides of the cutlets with the oil. *CONTINUED >*

Pork Katsu with Seasoned Rice continued

Prep tip: Instant rice is just rice that has been precooked and then dried, so it rehydrates quickly right in your Ninja. If you prefer to use leftover cooked rice instead, omit the water.

Super swap: Pork katsu is also great with Eggplant in Stir-Fry Sauce (page 144), Roasted Snap Peas and Scallions (page 80), or Roasted Green Beans and Shallots (page 135).

4. To prep the rice: In the Zone 2 basket, combine the rice, water, sesame oil, and soy sauce. Stir well to ensure all of the rice is submerged in the liquid.

5. To cook the pork and rice: Install a crisper plate in the Zone 1 basket. Place the pork in the basket and insert the basket in the unit. Insert the Zone 2 basket in the unit.

6. Select Zone 1, select AIR FRY, set the temperature to 390°F, and set the time to 15 minutes.

7. Select Zone 2, select BAKE, set the temperature to 350°F, and set the time to 10 minutes. Select SMART FINISH.™

8. Press START/PAUSE to begin cooking.

9. When the Zone 1 timer reads 10 minutes, press START/PAUSE. Remove the basket and use silicone-tipped tongs to flip the pork. Reinsert the basket and press START/PAUSE to resume cooking.

10. When cooking is complete, the pork should be crisp and cooked through and the rice tender.

11. Stir the sesame seeds and scallions into the rice. For the sauce to go with the pork, in a small bowl, whisk together the ketchup, Worcestershire sauce, oyster sauce, and sugar. Drizzle the sauce over the pork and serve with the hot rice.

Per serving: Calories: 563; Total fat: 20g; Saturated fat: 5.5g; Carbohydrates: 62g; Fiber: 1g; Protein: 34g; Sodium: 665mg

Garlic-Rosemary Pork Loin with Scalloped Potatoes and Cauliflower

SERVES 6

This herbed pork loin roast has tons of garlic and rosemary flavor that permeates the meat as it cooks and a delightfully crispy crust from being air-fried. It pairs wonderfully with tender scalloped potatoes and cauliflower for a fantastic Sunday supper or holiday meal.

NUT-FREE

Prep time: 15 minutes, plus 15 minutes to rest
Cook time: 50 minutes

FOR THE PORK LOIN

2 pounds pork loin roast

2 tablespoons vegetable oil

2 teaspoons dried thyme

2 teaspoons dried crushed rosemary

1 teaspoon minced garlic

¾ teaspoon kosher salt

FOR THE SCALLOPED POTATOES AND CAULIFLOWER

1 teaspoon vegetable oil

¾ pound Yukon Gold potatoes, peeled and very thinly sliced

1½ cups cauliflower florets

¼ teaspoon kosher salt

¼ teaspoon freshly ground black pepper

1 tablespoon very cold unsalted butter, grated

3 tablespoons all-purpose flour

1 cup whole milk

1 cup shredded Gruyère cheese

1. **To prep the pork loin:** Coat the pork with the oil. Season with thyme, rosemary, garlic, and salt.

2. **To prep the potatoes and cauliflower:** Brush the bottom and sides of the Zone 2 basket with the oil. Add one-third of the potatoes to the bottom of the basket and arrange in a single layer. Top with ½ cup of cauliflower florets. Sprinkle a third of the salt and black pepper on top. Scatter one-third of the butter on top and sprinkle on 1 tablespoon of flour. Repeat this step twice more for a total of three layers.

CONTINUED >

Super swap: Try this pork loin with Roasted Green Bean Casserole (page 96) or Baked Brown Sugar Acorn Squash (page 139).

3. Pour the milk over the layered potatoes and cauliflower; it should just cover the top layer. Top with the Gruyère.

4. **To cook the pork and scalloped vegetables:** Install a crisper plate in the Zone 1 basket. Place the pork loin in the basket and insert the basket in the unit. Insert the Zone 2 basket in the unit.

5. Select Zone 1, select AIR FRY, set the temperature to 390°F, and set the time to 50 minutes.

6. Select Zone 2, select BAKE, set the temperature to 350°F, and set the time to 45 minutes. Select SMART FINISH.™

7. Press START/PAUSE to begin cooking.

8. When cooking is complete, the pork will be cooked through (an instant-read thermometer should read 145°F) and the potatoes and cauliflower will be tender.

9. Let the pork rest for at least 15 minutes before slicing and serving with the scalloped vegetables.

Per serving: Calories: 439; Total fat: 25g; Saturated fat: 10g; Carbohydrates: 17g; Fiber: 1.5g; Protein: 37g; Sodium: 431mg

Pork Tenderloin with Brown Sugar–Pecan Sweet Potatoes

SERVES 4

Pork tenderloin is a long and narrow cut of meat that comes from the back of the pig. Don't confuse it with pork loin, which is more of a roast. Pork tenderloin is super lean, so roasting it in the air fryer ensures that you get a delicious and crispy exterior. I like to serve it with perfectly baked sweet potatoes stuffed with gooey brown sugar and pecans. If you'd like, you could also serve this with a store-bought pork gravy.

GLUTEN-FREE

Prep time: 5 minutes, plus 5 minutes to rest
Cook time: 45 minutes

FOR THE PORK TENDERLOIN

1½ pounds pork tenderloin

2 teaspoons vegetable oil

½ teaspoon kosher salt

½ teaspoon poultry seasoning

FOR THE SWEET POTATOES

4 teaspoons unsalted butter, at room temperature

2 tablespoons dark brown sugar

¼ cup chopped pecans

4 small sweet potatoes

1. **To prep the pork:** Coat the pork tenderloin with the oil, then rub with the salt and poultry seasoning.

2. **To prep the sweet potatoes:** In a small bowl, mix the butter, brown sugar, and pecans until well combined.

3. **To cook the pork and sweet potatoes:** Install a crisper plate in the Zone 1 basket. Place the pork tenderloin in the basket and insert the basket in the unit. Place the sweet potatoes in the Zone 2 basket and insert the basket in the unit.

4. Select Zone 1, select AIR FRY, set the temperature to 390°F, and set the time to 25 minutes.

CONTINUED >

Pork Tenderloin with Brown Sugar–Pecan Sweet Potatoes continued

Super swap: Pair this pork tenderloin with Roasted Asparagus and Mushroom Medley (page 112), Apple and Sage Stuffing (page 101), or Roasted Vegetable Salad (page 98).

5. Select Zone 2, select BAKE, set the temperature to 400ºF, and set the time to 45 minutes. Select SMART FINISH.™

6. Press START/PAUSE to begin cooking.

7. When the Zone 2 timer reads 10 minutes, press START/PAUSE. Remove the basket. Slice the sweet potatoes open lengthwise. Divide the pecan mixture among the potatoes. Reinsert the basket and press START/PAUSE to resume cooking.

8. When cooking is complete, the pork will be cooked through (an instant-read thermometer should read 145ºF) and the potatoes will be soft and their flesh fluffy.

9. Transfer the pork loin to a plate or cutting board and let rest for at least 5 minutes before slicing and serving.

Per serving: *Calories: 415; Total fat: 15g; Saturated fat: 4.5g; Carbohydrates: 33g; Fiber: 4.5g; Protein: 36g; Sodium: 284mg*

Barbecue Ribs with Roasted Green Beans and Shallots

SERVES 4

This dish is a barbecue lover's dream. The meaty ribs are tender and smoky, with tons of barbecue flavor from the dry rub. Served with your favorite barbecue sauce for dipping and a side of vibrant green beans with sweet roasted shallots, the flavor is elevated to a whole new level!

DAIRY-FREE, GLUTEN-FREE, NUT-FREE

Prep time: 5 minutes
Cook time: 40 minutes

FOR THE RIBS

1 tablespoon light brown sugar

1 tablespoon smoked paprika

1 tablespoon chili powder

2 teaspoons kosher salt

1 teaspoon freshly ground black pepper

1 teaspoon garlic powder

¼ teaspoon cayenne pepper (optional)

2 pounds pork ribs

1 cup barbecue sauce (your favorite), for serving

FOR THE GREEN BEANS AND SHALLOTS

1 pound green beans, trimmed

2 shallots, sliced

1 tablespoon olive oil

¼ teaspoon kosher salt

1. **To prep the ribs:** In a small bowl, combine the brown sugar, paprika, chili powder, salt, black pepper, garlic powder, and cayenne (if using).

2. Rub the spice blend all over both sides of the ribs.

3. **To prep the green beans and shallots:** In a large bowl, combine the green beans, shallots, and oil. Toss to coat. Season with the salt.

4. **To cook the ribs and vegetables:** Install a crisper plate in each of the two baskets. Place the ribs in the Zone 1 basket and insert the basket in the unit. Place the green beans in the Zone 2 basket and insert the basket in the unit.

CONTINUED >

Barbecue Ribs with Roasted Green Beans and Shallots continued

Super swap: You'll also love these ribs served with Street Corn (page 76), Crispy Kale Chips (page 74), or Warm Baked Potato Salad (page 93).

5. Select Zone 1, select AIR FRY, set the temperature to 375ºF, and set the time to 40 minutes.

6. Select Zone 2, select ROAST, set the temperature to 400ºF, and set the time to 20 minutes. Select SMART FINISH.™

7. Press START/PAUSE to begin cooking.

8. When the Zone 1 timer reads 10 minutes, press START/PAUSE. Increase the temperature of Zone 1 to 400ºF. Press START/PAUSE to resume cooking.

9. When cooking is complete, an instant-read thermometer inserted into the ribs should read 170ºF and the green beans should be tender-crisp. Serve topped with your favorite barbecue sauce.

Per serving: *Calories: 541; Total fat: 27g; Saturated fat: 9g; Carbohydrates: 48g; Fiber: 4.5g; Protein: 28g; Sodium: 1,291mg*

Italian Sausages with Peppers, Potatoes, and Onions

SERVES 4

This classic comfort food combination reminds me of one of my favorite meals growing up. Air-frying the sausages makes the outside nice and crispy while the inside stays super juicy. The peppers and onions add amazing flavor to this dish, and incorporating potatoes means you don't need to mess around with making pasta. Depending on your preference, you can use either hot or sweet sausages for this recipe.

DAIRY-FREE, GLUTEN-FREE, NUT-FREE

Prep time: 5 minutes
Cook time: 22 minutes

FOR THE PEPPERS, POTATOES, AND ONIONS

2 Yukon Gold potatoes, cut into ¼-inch slices

1 red bell pepper, sliced

1 yellow onion, sliced

¼ cup canned tomato sauce

1 tablespoon olive oil

1 teaspoon minced garlic

½ teaspoon dried oregano

¼ teaspoon kosher salt

FOR THE SAUSAGES

4 links Italian sausage

1. **To prep the peppers, potatoes, and onions:** In a large bowl, combine the potatoes, pepper, onion, tomato sauce, oil, garlic, oregano, and salt. Mix to combine.

2. **To cook the sausage and vegetables:** Install a crisper plate in each of the two baskets. Place the sausages in the Zone 1 basket and insert the basket in the unit. Place the potato mixture in the Zone 2 basket and insert the basket in the unit.

3. Select Zone 1, select AIR FRY, set the temperature to 390°F, and set the time to 22 minutes.

CONTINUED >

Italian Sausages with Peppers, Potatoes, and Onions continued

Super swap: Pair the Italian sausage links with Broiled Zucchini and Cherry Tomatoes (page 83), Roasted Asparagus and Mushroom Medley (page 112), or Crispy Zucchini Noodles (page 187).

4. Select Zone 2, select ROAST, set the temperature to 375ºF, and set the time to 20 minutes. Select SMART FINISH.™

5. Press START/PAUSE to begin cooking.

6. When cooking is complete, the sausages will be cooked through and the vegetables tender.

7. Slice the sausages into rounds, then mix them into the potato and pepper mixture. Serve.

Per serving: Calories: 335; Total fat: 22g; Saturated fat: 6.5g; Carbohydrates: 21g; Fiber: 2g; Protein: 15g; Sodium: 658mg

Curry-Crusted Lamb Chops with Baked Brown Sugar Acorn Squash

Curry is one of my favorite spices and it goes perfectly with the sweet, earthy flavors of lamb. The acorn squash adds another layer of comforting sweetness to this dish. Note that it is perfectly ok to eat the skin on acorn squash. This recipe is written to give you medium-rare lamb chops. If you prefer yours cooked more, increase the cooking time 1 to 3 minutes, depending on your preferred level of doneness.

GLUTEN-FREE, NUT-FREE

Prep time: 10 minutes, plus 5 minutes to rest
Cook time: 20 minutes

FOR THE LAMB CHOPS

4 lamb loin chops (4 ounces each)

1 tablespoon olive oil

2 teaspoons curry powder

¼ teaspoon kosher salt

FOR THE ACORN SQUASH

2 small acorn squash

4 teaspoons dark brown sugar

2 teaspoons salted butter

⅛ teaspoon kosher salt

1. **To prep the lamb chops:** Brush both sides of the lamb chops with the oil and season with the curry powder and salt.

2. **To prep the acorn squash:** Cut the squash in half through the stem end and remove the seeds. Place 1 teaspoon of brown sugar and ½ teaspoon of butter into the well of each squash half.

3. **To cook the lamb and squash:** Install a crisper plate in each of the two baskets. Place the lamb chops in the Zone 1 basket and insert the basket in the unit. Place the squash cut-side up in the Zone 2 basket and insert the basket in the unit.

4. Select Zone 1, select AIR FRY, set the temperature to 400°F, and set the timer to 15 minutes.

CONTINUED >

Curry-Crusted Lamb Chops with Baked Brown Sugar Acorn Squash continued

Super swap: Try these lamb chops with Roasted Vegetable Salad (page 98) or Roasted Asparagus and Mushroom Medley (page 112).

5. Select Zone 2, select BAKE, set the temperature to 400ºF, and set the time to 20 minutes. Select SMART FINISH.™

6. Press START/PAUSE to begin cooking.

7. When both timers read 5 minutes, press START/PAUSE. Remove the Zone 1 basket and use a pair of silicone-tipped tongs to flip the lamb chops. Reinsert the basket in the unit. Remove the Zone 2 basket and spoon the melted butter and sugar over the top edges of the squash. Reinsert the basket and press START/PAUSE to resume cooking.

8. When cooking is complete, the lamb should be cooked to your liking and the squash soft when pierced with a fork.

9. Remove the lamb chops from the basket and let rest for 5 minutes. Season the acorn squash with salt before serving.

Per serving: *Calories: 328; Total fat: 19g; Saturated fat: 7.5g; Carbohydrates: 23g; Fiber: 3g; Protein: 16g; Sodium: 172mg*

Blackened Mahimahi with Honey-Roasted Carrots, *page 146*

6

Seafood

Broiled Teriyaki Salmon with Eggplant in Stir-Fry Sauce

SERVES 4

Broiled salmon is one of my go-to meals after a long day. It only takes a few minutes to cook and it's incredibly rich in flavor. A tangy teriyaki sauce is a welcome addition to this dish. I paired this with air-fried eggplant topped with my favorite stir-fry sauce. The eggplant is so tender, you won't be able to stop eating it!

DAIRY-FREE, NUT-FREE

Prep time: 5 minutes
Cook time: 25 minutes

FOR THE TERIYAKI SALMON

4 salmon fillets (6 ounces each)

½ cup teriyaki sauce

3 scallions, sliced

FOR THE EGGPLANT

¼ cup reduced-sodium soy sauce

¼ cup packed light brown sugar

1 tablespoon minced fresh ginger

1 tablespoon minced garlic

2 teaspoons sesame oil

¼ teaspoon red pepper flakes

1 eggplant, peeled and cut into bite-size cubes

Nonstick cooking spray

1. **To prep the teriyaki salmon:** Brush the top of each salmon fillet with the teriyaki sauce.

2. **To prep the eggplant:** In a small bowl, whisk together the soy sauce, brown sugar, ginger, garlic, sesame oil, and red pepper flakes. Set the stir-fry sauce aside.

3. Spritz the eggplant cubes with cooking spray.

4. **To cook the salmon and eggplant:** Install a crisper plate in each of the two baskets. Place the salmon in a single layer in the Zone 1 basket and insert the basket in the unit. Place the eggplant in the Zone 2 basket and insert the basket in the unit.

5. Select Zone 1, select AIR BROIL, set the temperature to 450°F, and set the time to 8 minutes.

6. Select Zone 2, select AIR FRY, set the temperature to 390°F, and set the time to 25 minutes. Select SMART FINISH.™

7. Press START/PAUSE to begin cooking.

8. When the Zone 2 timer reads 5 minutes, press START/PAUSE. Remove the basket and pour the stir-fry sauce evenly over the eggplant. Shake or stir to coat the eggplant cubes in the sauce. Reinsert the basket and press START/PAUSE to resume cooking.

9. When cooking is complete, the salmon should be cooked to your liking and the eggplant tender and slightly caramelized. Serve hot.

Per serving: Calories: 499; Total fat: 22g; Saturated fat: 2g; Carbohydrates: 36g; Fiber: 3.5g; Protein: 42g; Sodium: 1,024mg

Super swap: Try this salmon with Seasoned Rice (page 129), Roasted Green Beans and Shallots (page 135), or Roasted Snap Peas and Scallions (page 80).

Blackened Mahimahi with Honey-Roasted Carrots

SERVES 4

Mahimahi is a firm white fish that works really well in the Foodi® Air Fryer. It's flavored here with a blackening seasoning to highlight its crispy exterior and add just a little bit of spice. The sweetness of the honey-roasted carrots helps tone down the heat, making it a great pairing with the fish. If any liquid collects under the crisper plate while the carrots cook, drizzle it over them before serving for even more flavor.

GLUTEN-FREE, NUT-FREE

Prep time: 5 minutes
Cook time: 30 minutes

FOR THE MAHIMAHI

4 mahimahi fillets (4 ounces each)

1 tablespoon olive oil

1 tablespoon blackening seasoning

Lemon wedges, for serving

FOR THE CARROTS

1 pound carrots, peeled and cut into ½-inch rounds

2 teaspoons vegetable oil

½ teaspoon kosher salt

¼ teaspoon freshly ground black pepper

1 tablespoon salted butter, cut into small pieces

1 tablespoon honey

2 tablespoons chopped fresh parsley

1. **To prep the mahimahi:** Brush both sides of the fish with the oil and sprinkle with the blackening seasoning.

2. **To prep the carrots:** In a large bowl, combine the carrots, oil, salt, and black pepper. Stir well to coat the carrots with the oil.

3. **To cook the mahimahi and carrots:** Install a crisper plate in each of the two baskets. Place the fish in the Zone 1 basket and insert the basket in the unit. Place the carrots in the Zone 2 basket and insert the basket in the unit.

4. Select Zone 1, select AIR FRY, set the temperature to 380°F, and set the timer to 14 minutes.

5. Select Zone 2, select ROAST, set the temperature to 400°F, and set the timer to 30 minutes. Select SMART FINISH.™

6. Press START/PAUSE to begin cooking.

7. When the Zone 2 timer reads 15 minutes, press START/PAUSE. Remove the basket and scatter the butter over the carrots, then drizzle them with the honey. Reinsert the basket and press START/PAUSE to resume cooking.

8. When cooking is complete, the fish should be cooked through and the carrots soft.

9. Stir the parsley into the carrots. Serve the fish with lemon wedges.

Per serving: Calories: 235; Total fat: 9.5g; Saturated fat: 3g; Carbohydrates: 15g; Fiber: 3g; Protein: 22g; Sodium: 672mg

Super swap: Try this mahimahi with Hush Puppies (page 164), Cacio e Pepe Brussels Sprouts (page 168), or Baked Macaroni and Cheese (page 148).

Parmesan-Crusted Fish Sticks with Baked Macaroni and Cheese

SERVES 4

This pairing is a bit of a calorie bomb, but it's worth every single bite. Fish sticks are a staple in many homes, but a touch of Parmesan cheese takes this home-made version to the next level. Use cod, haddock, or any other flaky white fish. The mac and cheese is made with Colby-Jack and a touch of cream cheese for a luxuriously rich and creamy sauce. You'll never believe homemade mac and cheese this good could be so easy to make—you don't even need to boil the pasta first!

NUT-FREE

Prep time: 10 minutes, plus 5 minutes to stand
Cook time: 25 minutes

Per serving: Calories: 903; Total fat: 51g; Saturated fat: 25g; Carbohydrates: 60g; Fiber: 2.5g; Protein: 48g; Sodium: 844mg

FOR THE FISH STICKS

- 1 pound cod or haddock fillets
- ½ cup all-purpose flour
- 2 large eggs
- ¼ teaspoon kosher salt
- ¼ teaspoon freshly ground black pepper
- ¾ cup panko bread crumbs
- ¼ cup grated Parmesan cheese
- Nonstick cooking spray

FOR THE MACARONI AND CHEESE

- 1½ cups elbow macaroni
- 1 cup whole milk
- ½ cup heavy (whipping) cream
- 8 ounces shredded Colby-Jack cheese
- 4 ounces cream cheese, at room temperature
- 1 teaspoon Dijon mustard
- ½ teaspoon kosher salt
- ½ teaspoon freshly ground black pepper

1. **To prep the fish sticks:** Cut the fish into sticks about 3 inches long and ¾ inch wide.

2. Set up a breading station with three small shallow bowls. Place the flour in the first bowl. In the second bowl, whisk the eggs and season with the salt and black pepper. Combine the panko and Parmesan in the third bowl.

3. Bread the fish sticks in this order: First, dip them into the flour, coating all sides. Then, dip into the beaten egg. Finally, coat them in the panko mixture, gently pressing the bread crumbs into the fish. Spritz each fish stick all over with cooking spray.

4. **To prep the macaroni and cheese:** Place the macaroni in the Zone 2 basket. Add the milk, cream, Colby-Jack, cream cheese, mustard, salt, and black pepper. Stir well to combine, ensuring the pasta is completely submerged in the liquid.

5. **To cook the fish sticks and macaroni and cheese:** Install a crisper plate in the Zone 1 basket. Arrange the fish sticks in a single layer in the basket (use a rack or cook in batches if necessary) and insert the basket in the unit. Insert the Zone 2 basket in the unit.

6. Select Zone 1, select AIR FRY, set the temperature to 390°F, and set the timer to 18 minutes.

7. Select Zone 2, select BAKE, set the temperature to 360°F, and set the timer to 25 minutes. Select SMART FINISH.™

8. Press START/PAUSE to begin cooking.

9. When the Zone 1 timer reads 3 minutes, press START/PAUSE. Remove the basket and use silicone-tipped tongs to gently flip over the fish sticks. Reinsert the basket and press START/PAUSE to resume cooking.

10. When cooking is complete, the fish sticks should be crisp and the macaroni tender.

11. Stir the macaroni and cheese and let stand for 5 minutes before serving. The sauce will thicken as it cools.

Super swap: These fish sticks also go great with Sweet Potato Fries (page 157), Roasted Lemon-Parmesan Broccoli (page 85), or Roasted Vegetable Salad (page 98).

Pecan-Crusted Catfish Nuggets with "Fried" Okra

SERVES 4

Catfish nuggets are a great alternative to traditional fried catfish. Soaking catfish in milk before breading helps mellow out its flavor, which can otherwise be fishy or heavy. It makes a huge difference in the flavor of the dish, so don't skip this step! Serve these crispy nuggets up with some tartar sauce or honey mustard and watch as everyone devours them. It doesn't get much better than this!

Prep time: 15 minutes, plus 1 hour to soak
Cook time: 17 minutes

FOR THE CATFISH NUGGETS

- 1 cup whole milk
- 1 pound fresh catfish nuggets (or cut-up fillets)
- 1 large egg
- 2 to 3 dashes Louisiana-style hot sauce (optional)
- ¼ cup finely chopped pecans
- ½ cup all-purpose flour
- Nonstick cooking spray
- Tartar sauce, for serving (optional)

FOR THE OKRA

- ½ cup fine yellow cornmeal
- ¼ cup all-purpose flour
- ½ teaspoon garlic powder
- ½ teaspoon paprika
- 1 teaspoon kosher salt
- 1 large egg
- 8 ounces frozen cut okra, thawed
- Nonstick cooking spray

1. **To prep the catfish:** Pour the milk into a large zip-top bag. Add the catfish and turn to coat. Set in the refrigerator to soak for at least 1 hour or up to overnight.

2. Remove the fish from the milk, shaking off any excess liquid.

3. In a shallow dish, whisk together the egg and hot sauce (if using). In a second shallow dish, combine the pecans and flour.

CONTINUED >

Super swap: Try these catfish nuggets with Baked Macaroni and Cheese (page 148), Seasoned Potato Wedges (page 155), or Hush Puppies (page 164).

4. Dip each piece of fish into the egg mixture, then into the nut mixture to coat. Gently press the nut mixture to adhere to the fish. Spritz each nugget with cooking spray.

5. **To prep the okra:** Set up a breading station with two small shallow bowls. In the first bowl, stir together the cornmeal, flour, garlic powder, paprika, and salt. In the second bowl, whisk the egg.

6. Dip the okra first in the cornmeal mixture, then the egg, then back into the cornmeal. Spritz with cooking spray.

7. **To cook the catfish and okra:** Install a crisper plate in each of the two baskets. Place the fish in a single layer in the Zone 1 basket and insert the basket in the unit. Place the okra in the Zone 2 basket and insert the basket in the unit.

8. Select Zone 1, select AIR FRY, set the temperature to 390°F, and set the timer to 17 minutes.

9. Select Zone 2, select AIR FRY, set the temperature to 400°F, and set the timer to 12 minutes. Select SMART FINISH.™

10. Press START/PAUSE to begin cooking.

11. When cooking is complete, the fish should be cooked through and the okra golden brown and crispy. Serve hot.

Per serving: Calories: 414; Total fat: 24g; Saturated fat: 2.5g; Carbohydrates: 30g; Fiber: 3g; Protein: 23g; Sodium: 569mg

Tilapia with Mojo and Crispy Plantains

SERVES 4

Mojo is a classic Cuban sauce that's tangy and garlicky, making it the perfect pairing for tilapia. It's traditionally made with sour oranges, but a combination of orange juice and lime juice provides a similar citrusy pop. The sweet and crispy plantains go great with any leftover sauce.

DAIRY-FREE, NUT-FREE

Prep time: 10 minutes, plus 15 minutes to soak
Cook time: 30 minutes

FOR THE TILAPIA

- 4 tilapia fillets (6 ounces each)
- 2 tablespoons all-purpose flour
- Nonstick cooking spray
- ¼ cup freshly squeezed orange juice
- 3 tablespoons fresh lime juice
- 2 tablespoons olive oil
- 1 tablespoon minced garlic
- ½ teaspoon ground cumin
- ¼ teaspoon kosher salt

FOR THE PLANTAINS

- 1 large green plantain
- 2 cups cold water
- 2 teaspoons kosher salt
- Nonstick cooking spray

1. **To prep the tilapia:** Dust both sides of the tilapia fillets with the flour, then spritz with cooking spray.

2. In a small bowl, whisk together the orange juice, lime juice, oil, garlic, cumin, and salt. Set the mojo sauce aside.

3. **To prep the plantains:** Cut the ends from the plantain, then remove and discard the peel. Slice the plantain into 1-inch rounds.

4. In a large bowl, combine the water, salt, and plantains. Let soak for 15 minutes.

5. Drain the plantains and pat them dry with paper towels. Spray with cooking spray.

CONTINUED >

Super swap: This tilapia is also delicious with Honey-Roasted Carrots (page 146), Mexican Rice (page 116), and Tortilla Chips (page 64).

6. To cook the tilapia and plantains: Install a crisper plate in each of the two baskets. Place the tilapia in a single layer in the Zone 1 basket (work in batches if needed) and insert the basket in the unit. Place the plantains in the Zone 2 basket and insert the basket in the unit.

7. Select Zone 1, select AIR FRY, set the temperature to 390°F, and set the timer to 10 minutes.

8. Select Zone 2, select AIR FRY, set the temperature to 390°F, and set the timer to 30 minutes. Select SMART FINISH.™

9. Press START/PAUSE to begin cooking.

10. When the Zone 2 timer reads 10 minutes, press START/PAUSE. Remove the basket and use silicone-tipped tongs to transfer the plantains, which should be tender, to a cutting board. Use the bottom of a heavy glass to smash each plantain flat. Spray both sides with cooking spray and place them back in the basket. Reinsert the basket and press START/PAUSE to resume cooking.

11. When the Zone 1 timer reads 5 minutes, press START/PAUSE. Remove the basket. Spoon half of the mojo sauce over the tilapia. Reinsert the basket and press START/PAUSE to resume cooking.

12. When cooking is complete, the fish should be cooked through and the plantains crispy. Serve the tilapia and plantains with the remaining mojo sauce for dipping.

Per serving: Calories: 380; Total fat: 21g; Saturated fat: 2g; Carbohydrates: 20g; Fiber: 1g; Protein: 35g; Sodium: 217mg

"Fried" Fish with Seasoned Potato Wedges

SERVES 4

Classic fish and chips is a common request when it comes to air fryer recipes. Getting a traditional battered exterior on the fish can be tricky, but with a little practice it isn't too difficult. The trick is to line the bottom of the basket with parchment or aluminum foil so the batter doesn't drip through and to handle the fish very carefully until the batter is completely cooked.

DAIRY-FREE, NUT-FREE

Prep time: 10 minutes, plus 10 minutes to rest
Cook time: 30 minutes

FOR THE FISH

4 cod fillets (6 ounces each)

4 tablespoons all-purpose flour, divided

¼ cup cornstarch

1 teaspoon baking powder

¼ teaspoon kosher salt

⅓ cup lager-style beer or sparkling water

Tartar sauce, cocktail sauce, or malt vinegar, for serving (optional)

FOR THE POTATOES

4 russet potatoes

2 tablespoons vegetable oil

½ teaspoon paprika

½ teaspoon kosher salt

¼ teaspoon garlic powder

¼ teaspoon freshly ground black pepper

1. **To prep the fish:** Pat the fish dry with a paper towel and coat lightly with 2 tablespoons of flour.

2. In a shallow dish, combine the remaining 2 tablespoons of flour, the cornstarch, baking powder, and salt. Stir in the beer to form a thick batter.

3. Dip the fish in the batter to coat both sides, then let rest on a cutting board for 10 minutes.

4. **To prep the potatoes:** Cut each potato in half lengthwise, then cut each half into 4 wedges.

CONTINUED >

Super swap: You'll also love this "fried" fish with Sweet Potato Fries (page 157) or Crispy Kale Chips (page 74).

5. In a large bowl, combine the potatoes and oil. Toss well to fully coat the potatoes. Add the paprika, salt, garlic powder, and black pepper and toss well to coat.

6. **To cook the fish and potato wedges:** Install a crisper plate in each of the two baskets. Place a piece of parchment paper or aluminum foil over the plate in the Zone 1 basket. Place the fish in the basket and insert the basket in the unit. Place the potato wedges in a single layer in the Zone 2 basket and insert the basket in the unit.

7. Select Zone 1, select AIR FRY, set the temperature to 400°F, and set the timer to 13 minutes.

8. Select Zone 2, select AIR FRY, set the temperature to 400°F, and set the timer to 30 minutes. Select SMART FINISH.™

9. Press START/PAUSE to begin cooking.

10. When the Zone 1 timer reads 5 minutes, press START/PAUSE. Remove the basket and use a silicone spatula to carefully flip the fish over. Reinsert the basket and press START/PAUSE to resume cooking.

11. When cooking is complete, the fish should be cooked through and the potatoes crispy outside and tender inside. Serve hot with tartar sauce, cocktail sauce, or malt vinegar (if using).

Per serving: *Calories: 360; Total fat: 8g; Saturated fat: 1g; Carbohydrates: 40g; Fiber: 2g; Protein: 30g; Sodium: 302mg*

Shrimp Po'Boys with Sweet Potato Fries

SERVES 4

I fell in love with po'boys on a trip to New Orleans a few years ago. I still remember being blown away by the different textures in that first bite, from crispy fried shrimp to creamy rémoulade sauce to the juicy tomato. This Foodi® Air Fryer version is a great way to relive that trip any time I want.

NUT-FREE

Prep time: 20 minutes, plus 10 minutes to sit
Cook time: 30 minutes

FOR THE SHRIMP PO'BOYS
½ cup buttermilk

1 tablespoon Louisiana-style hot sauce

¾ cup all-purpose flour

½ cup cornmeal

½ teaspoon kosher salt

½ teaspoon paprika

½ teaspoon garlic powder

½ teaspoon freshly ground black pepper

1 pound peeled medium shrimp, thawed if frozen

Nonstock cooking spray

½ cup store-bought rémoulade sauce

4 French bread rolls, halved lengthwise

½ cup shredded lettuce

1 tomato, sliced

FOR THE SWEET POTATO FRIES
2 medium sweet potatoes

2 teaspoons vegetable oil

¼ teaspoon garlic powder

¼ teaspoon paprika

¼ teaspoon kosher salt

1. **To prep the shrimp:** In a medium bowl, combine the buttermilk and hot sauce. In a shallow bowl, combine the flour, cornmeal, salt, paprika, garlic powder, and black pepper.

2. Add the shrimp to the buttermilk and stir to coat. Remove the shrimp, letting the excess buttermilk drip off, then add to the cornmeal mixture to coat.

3. Spritz the breaded shrimp with cooking spray, then let sit for 10 minutes.

CONTINUED >

Super swap: These po'boys also pair with "Fried" Okra (page 150), Barbecue Potato Chips (page 114), or Crispy Kale Chips (page 74).

4. To prep the sweet potatoes: Peel the sweet potatoes and cut them lengthwise into ¼-inch-thick sticks (like shoestring fries).

5. In a large bowl, combine the sweet potatoes, oil, garlic powder, paprika, and salt. Toss to coat.

6. To cook the shrimp and fries: Install a crisper plate in each of the two baskets. Place the shrimp in the Zone 1 basket and insert the basket in the unit. Place the sweet potatoes in a single layer in the Zone 2 basket and insert the basket in the unit.

7. Select Zone 1, select AIR FRY, set the temperature to 390°F, and set the timer to 13 minutes.

8. Select Zone 2, select AIR FRY, set the temperature to 400°F, and set the timer to 30 minutes. Select SMART FINISH.™

9. Press START/PAUSE to begin cooking.

10. When cooking is complete, the shrimp should be golden and cooked through and the sweet potato fries crisp.

11. Spread the rémoulade on the cut sides of the rolls. Divide the lettuce and tomato among the rolls, then top with the fried shrimp. Serve with the sweet potato fries on the side.

Per serving: Calories: 669; Total fat: 22g; Saturated fat: 2g; Carbohydrates: 86g; Fiber: 3.5g; Protein: 33g; Sodium: 1,020mg

Bang Bang Shrimp with Roasted Bok Choy

SERVES 4

Shrimp cooks super fast in the Foodi® Air Fryer, so this dish is on the table in just minutes. The shrimp are coated with a crispy batter that comes out so light and crunchy! Tossed in a creamy, spicy sauce, this dish is sure to be a hit. The bright flavor of the bok choy, a tender leafy vegetable with a mild cabbage-like flavor, provides a nice contrast to the rich shrimp.

DAIRY-FREE, NUT-FREE

Prep time: 15 minutes
Cook time: 13 minutes

FOR THE BANG BANG SHRIMP

½ cup all-purpose flour

2 large eggs

1 cup panko bread crumbs

1 pound peeled shrimp (tails removed), thawed if frozen

Nonstick cooking spray

½ cup mayonnaise

¼ cup Thai sweet chili sauce

¼ teaspoon sriracha

FOR THE BOK CHOY

1 tablespoon reduced-sodium soy sauce

1 teaspoon minced garlic

1 teaspoon sesame oil

1 teaspoon minced fresh ginger

1½ pounds baby bok choy, halved lengthwise

1 tablespoon toasted sesame seeds

1. **To prep the shrimp:** Set up a breading station with three small shallow bowls. Place the flour in the first bowl. In the second bowl, whisk the eggs. Place the panko in the third bowl.

2. Bread the shrimp in this order: First, dip them into the flour, coating both sides. Then, dip into the beaten egg. Finally, coat them in the panko, gently pressing the bread crumbs to adhere to the shrimp. Spritz both sides of the shrimp with cooking spray.

3. **To prep the bok choy:** In a small bowl, whisk together the soy sauce, garlic, sesame oil, and ginger.

4. To cook the shrimp and bok choy: Install a crisper plate in the Zone 1 basket. Place the shrimp in the basket in a single layer and insert the basket in the unit. Place the boy choy cut-side up in the Zone 2 basket. Pour the sauce over the bok choy and insert the basket in the unit.

5. Select Zone 1, select AIR FRY, set the temperature to 390°F, and set the timer to 13 minutes.

6. Select Zone 2, select BAKE, set the temperature to 370°F, and set the timer to 8 minutes. Select SMART FINISH.™

7. Press START/PAUSE to begin cooking.

8. When cooking is complete, the shrimp should be cooked through and golden brown and the bok choy soft and slightly caramelized.

9. In a large bowl, whisk together the mayonnaise, sweet chili sauce, and sriracha. Add the shrimp and toss to coat.

10. Sprinkle the bok choy with the sesame seeds and serve hot alongside the shrimp.

Per serving: Calories: 534; Total fat: 33g; Saturated fat: 4g; Carbohydrates: 29g; Fiber: 3g; Protein: 31g; Sodium: 789mg

Super swap: Try this shrimp dish with Seasoned Rice (page 129), Eggplant in Stir-Fry Sauce (page 144), or Sweet Chili Brussels Sprouts (page 110).

Garlic Shrimp with Pasta Alfredo

SERVES 4

This creamy Alfredo sauce is so satisfying! No-boil lasagna noodles are designed to cook by absorbing the sauce around them, so they come out tender and flavorful without having to be cooked first on the stovetop. Garlicky shrimp are the perfect accompaniment. If you want even more flavor and a little heat in the shrimp, add ½ teaspoon Cajun seasoning along with the oil and garlic.

NUT-FREE

Prep time: 10 minutes
Cook time: 40 minutes

FOR THE GARLIC SHRIMP

1 pound peeled small shrimp, thawed if frozen

1 tablespoon olive oil

1 tablespoon minced garlic

¼ teaspoon sea salt

¼ cup chopped fresh parsley

FOR THE PASTA ALFREDO

8 ounces no-boil lasagna noodles

2 cups whole milk

¼ cup heavy (whipping) cream

2 tablespoons unsalted butter, cut into small pieces

1 tablespoon minced garlic

½ teaspoon kosher salt

¼ teaspoon freshly ground black pepper

½ cup grated Parmesan cheese

1. **To prep the garlic shrimp:** In a large bowl, combine the shrimp, oil, garlic, and salt.

2. **To prep the pasta alfredo:** Break the lasagna noodles into 2-inch pieces. Add the milk to the Zone 2 basket, then add the noodles, cream, butter, garlic, salt, and black pepper. Stir well and ensure the pasta is fully submerged in the liquid.

3. **To cook the shrimp and pasta:** Install a crisper plate in the Zone 1 basket. Place the shrimp in the basket and insert the basket in the unit. Insert the Zone 2 basket in the unit.

4. Select Zone 1, select AIR FRY, set the temperature to 390ºF, and set the timer to 13 minutes.

5. Select Zone 2, select BAKE, set the temperature to 360ºF, and set the timer to 40 minutes. Select SMART FINISH.™

6. Press START/PAUSE to begin cooking.

7. When the Zone 2 timer reads 20 minutes, press START/PAUSE. Remove the basket and stir the pasta. Reinsert the basket and press START/PAUSE to resume cooking.

8. When cooking is complete, the shrimp will be cooked through and the pasta tender.

9. Transfer the pasta to a serving dish and stir in the Parmesan. Top with the shrimp and parsley.

Per serving: Calories: 542; Total fat: 23g; Saturated fat: 11g; Carbohydrates: 52g; Fiber: 2g; Protein: 34g; Sodium: 643mg

Super swap: Try serving this garlic shrimp with Mexican Rice (page 116), Roasted Lemon-Parmesan Broccoli (page 85), or Crispy Zucchini Noodles (page 187).

Broiled Crab Cakes with Hush Puppies

SERVES 4

When I lived in Maryland, I ate crab cakes pretty much every chance I had. Now that I'm in New York, I have to take matters into my own hands by making them myself. Mixing the crab and shaping the cakes is a little labor-intensive, but they're so worth it. I paired these with air-fried hush puppies—sweet and crisp corn fritters that are great for serving with fried fish.

NUT-FREE

Prep time: 20 minutes, plus 30 minutes to chill
Cook time: 15 minutes

FOR THE CRAB CAKES

2 large eggs

2 tablespoons Dijon mustard

2 teaspoons Worcestershire sauce

1 teaspoon Old Bay seasoning

¼ teaspoon paprika

¼ cup cracker crumbs (about 9 crackers)

1 pound lump crab meat

2 teaspoons vegetable oil

FOR THE HUSH PUPPIES

½ cup all-purpose flour

⅓ cup yellow cornmeal

3 tablespoons sugar

¼ teaspoon kosher salt

¼ teaspoon baking powder

1 large egg

½ cup whole milk

Nonstick cooking spray

1. **To prep the crab cakes:** In a large bowl, whisk together the eggs, mustard, Worcestershire, Old Bay, and paprika until smooth. Stir in the cracker crumbs until fully incorporated, then fold in the crab meat. Refrigerate the crab mixture for 30 minutes.

2. Divide the crab mixture into 8 equal portions. With damp hands, press each portion gently into a loose patty. Brush both sides of each patty with the oil.

3. **To prep the hush puppies:** In a large bowl, combine the flour, cornmeal, sugar, salt, and baking powder. Stir in the egg and milk to form a stiff batter.

4. Roll the batter into 8 balls. Spritz each hush puppy with cooking spray.

5. To cook the crab cakes and hush puppies: Install a crisper plate in each of the two baskets. Place the crab cakes in a single layer in the Zone 1 basket and insert the basket in the unit. Line the Zone 2 plate with aluminum foil and spray the foil with cooking spray. Arrange the hush puppies on the foil and insert the basket in the unit.

6. Select Zone 1, select AIR BROIL, set the temperature to 400°F, and set the timer to 15 minutes.

7. Select Zone 2, select AIR FRY, set the temperature to 400°F, and set the timer to 7 minutes. Select SMART FINISH.™

8. Press START/PAUSE to begin cooking.

9. When cooking is complete, the crab cakes and hush puppies will be golden brown and cooked through. Serve hot.

Per serving: Calories: 403; Total fat: 16g; Saturated fat: 2g; Carbohydrates: 40g; Fiber: 1g; Protein: 27g; Sodium: 872mg

Super swap: Enjoy these crab cakes with Roasted Bok Choy (page 160), Broiled Zucchini and Cherry Tomatoes (page 83), or Zucchini Chips (page 184).

Air-Fried Tofu Cutlets with Cacio e Pepe Brussels Sprouts, *page 168*

7

Vegetarian Mains

Air-Fried Tofu Cutlets with Cacio e Pepe Brussels Sprouts

SERVES 4

These Italian-inspired tofu cutlets are a great way to add lean protein to your plate. The tofu is crispy on the outside and tender on the inside, like a perfect cutlet should be. For the best texture, freeze the tofu, then thaw and press out as much liquid as you can. This gives it a firmer, chewier texture similar to meat. Roasted Brussels sprouts tossed with pecorino cheese and freshly ground black pepper make a flavor-packed side dish.

NUT-FREE, VEGETARIAN

Prep time: 15 minutes
Cook time: 25 minutes

FOR THE TOFU CUTLETS

1 (14-ounce) package extra-firm tofu, drained

1 cup panko bread crumbs

¼ cup grated pecorino romano or Parmesan cheese

1 teaspoon garlic powder

1 teaspoon onion powder

¼ teaspoon kosher salt

1 tablespoon vegetable oil

4 lemon wedges, for serving

FOR THE BRUSSELS SPROUTS

1 pound Brussels sprouts, trimmed

1 tablespoon vegetable oil

2 tablespoons grated pecorino romano or Parmesan cheese

½ teaspoon freshly ground black pepper, plus more to taste

¼ teaspoon kosher salt

1. **To prep the tofu:** Cut the tofu horizontally into 4 slabs.

2. In a shallow bowl, mix together the panko, cheese, garlic powder, onion powder, and salt. Press both sides of each tofu slab into the panko mixture. Drizzle both sides with the oil.

3. **To prep the Brussels sprouts:** Cut the Brussels sprouts in half through the root end.

4. In a large bowl, combine the Brussels sprouts and olive oil. Mix to coat.

5. To cook the tofu cutlets and Brussels sprouts:
Install a crisper plate in each of the two baskets. Place the tofu cutlets in a single layer in the Zone 1 basket and insert the basket in the unit. Place the Brussels sprouts in the Zone 2 basket and insert the basket in the unit.

6. Select Zone 1, select AIR FRY, set the temperature to 400°F, and set the timer to 20 minutes.

7. Select Zone 2, select ROAST, set the temperature to 400°F, and set the timer to 25 minutes. Select SMART FINISH.™

8. Press START/PAUSE to begin cooking.

9. When both timers read 5 minutes, press START/PAUSE. Remove the Zone 1 basket and use a pair of silicone-tipped tongs to flip the tofu cutlets, then reinsert the basket in the unit. Remove the Zone 2 basket and sprinkle the cheese and black pepper over the Brussels sprouts. Reinsert the basket and press START/PAUSE to resume cooking.

10. When cooking is complete, the tofu should be crisp and the Brussels sprouts tender and beginning to brown.

11. Squeeze the lemon wedges over the tofu cutlets. Stir the Brussels sprouts, then season with the salt and additional black pepper to taste.

Per serving: Calories: 319; Total fat: 15g; Saturated fat: 3.5g; Carbohydrates: 27g; Fiber: 6g; Protein: 20g; Sodium: 402mg

Super swap: Tofu cutlets also pair well with Roasted Asparagus and Mushroom Medley (page 112), Buttery Roasted Radishes (page 72), or Pasta Alfredo (page 162).

Jerk Tofu with Roasted Cabbage

SERVES 4

If you're looking for a quick and easy weeknight dinner, this tofu recipe will hit the spot. Tofu doesn't have much flavor on its own, but it's the perfect canvas for bright and vibrant jerk seasoning. This dish is great for those looking to eat less meat but who still crave Caribbean-inspired flavors.

DAIRY-FREE, NUT-FREE, VEGAN

Prep time: 10 minutes, plus 15 minutes to marinate
Cook time: 20 minutes

FOR THE JERK TOFU
1 (14-ounce) package extra-firm tofu, drained

1 tablespoon apple cider vinegar

1 tablespoon reduced-sodium soy sauce

2 tablespoons jerk seasoning

Juice of 1 lime

½ teaspoon kosher salt

2 tablespoons olive oil

FOR THE CABBAGE
1 (14-ounce) bag coleslaw mix

1 red bell pepper, thinly sliced

2 scallions, thinly sliced

2 tablespoons water

3 garlic cloves, minced

¼ teaspoon fresh thyme leaves

¼ teaspoon onion powder

¼ teaspoon kosher salt

¼ teaspoon freshly ground black pepper

1. **To prep the jerk tofu:** Cut the tofu horizontally into 4 slabs.

2. In a shallow dish (big enough to hold the tofu slabs), whisk together the vinegar, soy sauce, jerk seasoning, lime juice, and salt.

3. Place the tofu in the marinade and turn to coat both sides. Cover and marinate for at least 15 minutes (or up to overnight in the refrigerator).

4. **To prep the cabbage:** In the Zone 2 basket, combine the coleslaw, bell pepper, scallions, water, garlic, thyme, onion powder, salt, and black pepper.

5. To cook the tofu and cabbage: Install a crisper plate in the Zone 1 basket and add the tofu in a single layer. Brush the tofu with the oil and insert the basket in the unit. Insert the Zone 2 basket in the unit.

6. Select Zone 1, select AIR FRY, set the temperature to 390°F, and set the timer to 15 minutes.

7. Select Zone 2, select ROAST, set the temperature to 330°F, and set the timer to 20 minutes. Select SMART FINISH.™

8. Press START/PAUSE to begin cooking.

9. When both timers read 5 minutes, press START/PAUSE. Remove the Zone 1 basket and use silicone-tipped tongs to flip the tofu. Reinsert the basket in the unit. Remove the Zone 2 basket and stir the cabbage. Reinsert the basket and press START/PAUSE to resume cooking.

10. When cooking is complete, the tofu will be crispy and browned around the edges and the cabbage soft.

11. Transfer the tofu to four plates and serve with the cabbage on the side.

Per serving: *Calories: 220; Total fat: 12g; Saturated fat: 1.5g; Carbohydrates: 21g; Fiber: 5g; Protein: 12g; Sodium: 817mg*

Prep tip: Buying bagged coleslaw mix saves you the effort of shredding cabbage and carrots.

Super swap: Try this jerk tofu with Sweet Potato Fries (page 157), Baked Macaroni and Cheese (page 148), or Hush Puppies (page 164).

Potato and Parsnip Latkes with Baked Apples

I have a few recipes for latkes, but this one is my favorite. A mix of potatoes and parsnips adds a hint of sweetness and a slight peppery flavor. Air-frying them makes them so crispy! I love pairing the latkes with apples that get baked down into a chunky applesauce. If you prefer, they also pair beautifully with sour cream.

NUT-FREE, VEGETARIAN

Prep time: 20 minutes, plus 5 minutes to sit
Cook time: 20 minutes

FOR THE LATKES

2 medium russet potatoes, peeled

1 large egg white

2 tablespoons all-purpose flour

¼ teaspoon garlic powder

¼ teaspoon kosher salt

¼ teaspoon freshly ground black pepper

1 medium parsnip, peeled and shredded

2 scallions, thinly sliced

2 tablespoons vegetable oil

FOR THE BAKED APPLES

2 Golden Delicious apples, peeled and diced

2 tablespoons granulated sugar

2 teaspoons unsalted butter, cut into small pieces

1. **To prep the latkes:** Grate the potatoes using the large holes of a box grater. Squeeze as much liquid out of the potatoes as you can into a large bowl. Set the potatoes aside in a separate bowl.

2. Let the potato liquid sit for 5 minutes, during which time the potato starch will settle to the bottom of the bowl. Pour off the water that has risen to the top, leaving the potato starch in the bowl.

3. Add the egg white, flour, salt, and black pepper to the potato starch to form a thick paste. Add the potatoes, parsnip, and scallions and mix well. Divide the mixture into 4 patties. Brush both sides of each patty with the oil.

Potato and Parsnip Latkes with Baked Apples continued

Variation: For a sweeter take on these latkes, make them with shredded sweet potato.

Super swap: I also like these latkes paired with Roasted Vegetable Salad (page 98). They're also great for breakfast with Spinach and Red Pepper Egg Cups (page 28).

4. To prep the baked apples: Place the apples in the Zone 2 basket. Sprinkle the sugar and butter over the top.

5. To cook the latkes and apples: Install a crisper plate in the Zone 1 basket. Place the latkes in the basket in a single layer, then insert the basket in the unit. Insert the Zone 2 basket in the unit.

6. Select Zone 1, select AIR FRY, set the temperature to 375°F, and set the timer to 15 minutes.

7. Select Zone 2, select BAKE, set the temperature to 330°F, and set the timer to 20 minutes. Select SMART FINISH.™

8. Press START/PAUSE to begin cooking.

9. When both timers read 5 minutes, press START/PAUSE. Remove the Zone 1 basket and use silicone-tipped tongs or a spatula to flip the latkes. Reinsert the basket in the unit. Remove the Zone 2 basket and gently mash the apples with a fork or the back of a spoon. Reinsert the basket and press START/PAUSE to resume cooking.

10. When cooking is complete, the latkes should be golden brown and cooked through and the apples very soft.

11. Transfer the latkes to a plate and serve with apples on the side.

Per serving: *Calories: 257; Total fat: 9g; Saturated fat: 2g; Carbohydrates: 42g; Fiber: 5.5g; Protein: 4g; Sodium: 91mg*

Spanakopita Rolls with Mediterranean Vegetable Salad

SERVES 4

These rolls, stuffed with spinach and feta, are a fun spin on Greek spinach pie. They come together in just about 30 minutes, making them perfect for weeknight meals or easy entertaining. Pair them with this flavorful roasted eggplant and chickpea salad dressed with Greek vinaigrette for a simple but satisfying meal.

NUT-FREE, VEGETARIAN

Prep time: 15 minutes
Cook time: 15 minutes

FOR THE SPANAKOPITA ROLLS

1 (10-ounce) package chopped frozen spinach, thawed

4 ounces feta cheese, crumbled

2 large eggs

1 teaspoon dried oregano

½ teaspoon freshly ground black pepper

12 sheets phyllo dough, thawed

Nonstick cooking spray

FOR THE ROASTED VEGETABLES

1 medium eggplant, diced

1 small red onion, cut into 8 wedges

1 red bell pepper, sliced

2 tablespoons olive oil

FOR THE SALAD

1 (15-ounce) can chickpeas, drained and rinsed

¼ cup chopped fresh parsley

¼ cup olive oil

¼ cup red wine vinegar

2 garlic cloves, minced

½ teaspoon dried oregano

¼ teaspoon kosher salt

¼ teaspoon freshly ground black pepper

1. **To prep the spanakopita rolls:** Squeeze as much liquid from the spinach as you can and place the spinach in a large bowl. Add the feta, eggs, oregano, and black pepper. Mix well.

2. Lay one sheet of phyllo on a clean work surface and mist it with cooking spray. Place another sheet of phyllo directly on top of the first sheet and mist it with cooking spray. Repeat with a third sheet. *CONTINUED >*

Spanakopita Rolls with Mediterranean Vegetable Salad continued

Prep tip: Frozen spinach is already wilted, so you don't need to precook it before using it to make these rolls.

Super swap: Pair spanakopita rolls with Lemon-Feta Baby Potatoes (page 126) or Crispy Kale Chips (page 74).

3. Spoon one-quarter of the spinach mixture along one short side of the phyllo. Fold the long sides in over the spinach, then roll up it like a burrito.

4. Repeat this process with the remaining phyllo sheets and spinach mixture to form 4 rolls.

5. **To prep the vegetables:** In a large bowl, combine the eggplant, onion, bell pepper, and oil. Mix well.

6. **To cook the rolls and vegetables:** Install a crisper plate in each of the two baskets. Place the spanakopita rolls seam-side down in the Zone 1 basket, and spritz the rolls with cooking spray. Place the vegetables in the Zone 2 basket and insert both baskets in the unit.

7. Select Zone 1, select AIR FRY, set the temperature to 375°F, and set the timer to 10 minutes.

Select Zone 2, select ROAST, set the temperature to 375°F, and set the timer to 15 minutes. Select SMART FINISH.™

8. Press START/PAUSE to begin cooking.

9. When the Zone 1 timer reads 3 minutes, press START/PAUSE. Remove the basket and use silicone-tipped tongs or a spatula to flip the spanakopita rolls. Reinsert the basket and press START/PAUSE to resume cooking.

10. When cooking is complete, the rolls should be crisp and golden brown and the vegetables tender.

11. **To assemble the salad:** Transfer the roasted vegetables to a large bowl. Stir in the chickpeas and parsley.

12. In a small bowl, whisk together the oil, vinegar, garlic, oregano, salt, and black pepper. Pour the dressing over the vegetables and toss to coat. Serve warm.

Per serving: *Calories: 739; Total fat: 51g; Saturated fat: 8g; Carbohydrates: 67g; Fiber: 11g; Protein: 21g; Sodium: 806mg*

Balsamic-Glazed Tofu with Roasted Butternut Squash

SERVES 4

Tofu is perfect for absorbing the flavor of this simple balsamic marinade. I use firm tofu for this recipe—I love the contrast of the crisp, caramelized edges with the slightly creamy center. You'll love how well the sweet squash complements the tangy marinade.

DAIRY-FREE, NUT-FREE, VEGAN

Prep time: 10 minutes, plus 20 minutes to marinate
Cook time: 40 minutes

FOR THE BALSAMIC TOFU

2 tablespoons balsamic vinegar

1 tablespoon maple syrup

1 teaspoon soy sauce

1 teaspoon Dijon mustard

1 (14-ounce) package firm tofu, drained and cut into large cubes

1 tablespoon canola oil

FOR THE BUTTERNUT SQUASH

1 small butternut squash

1 tablespoon canola oil

1 teaspoon light brown sugar

¼ teaspoon kosher salt

¼ teaspoon freshly ground black pepper

1. **To prep the balsamic tofu:** In a large bowl, whisk together the vinegar, maple syrup, soy sauce, and mustard. Add the tofu and stir to coat. Cover and marinate for at least 20 minutes (or up to overnight in the refrigerator).

2. **To prep the butternut squash:** Peel the squash and cut in half lengthwise. Remove and discard the seeds. Cut the squash crosswise into ½-inch-thick slices.

3. Brush the squash pieces with the oil, then sprinkle with the brown sugar, salt, and black pepper.

4. **To cook the tofu and squash:** Install a crisper plate in each of the two baskets. Place the tofu in the Zone 1 basket, drizzle with the oil, and insert the basket in the unit. Place the squash in the Zone 2 basket and insert the basket in the unit.

5. Select Zone 1, select AIR FRY, set the temperature to 400ºF, and set the timer to 10 minutes.

6. Select Zone 2, select ROAST, set the temperature to 400ºF, and set the timer to 40 minutes. Select SMART FINISH.™

7. Press START/PAUSE to begin cooking.

8. When cooking is complete, the tofu will have begun to crisp and brown around the edges and the squash should be tender. Serve hot.

Per serving: Calories: 253; Total fat: 11g; Saturated fat: 1g; Carbohydrates: 30g; Fiber: 4.5g; Protein: 11g; Sodium: 237mg

Prep tip: You can substitute your favorite balsamic dressing for the homemade marinade.

Super swap: Try balsamic-glazed tofu with Roasted Green Beans and Shallots (page 135), Turkey Meatloaf with Veggie Medley (page 103), or Garlicky Roasted Broccoli (page 108).

Satay-Style Tempeh with Corn Fritters

SERVES 4

Tempeh, which is made from fermented soybeans, has a hearty texture and a nutty, earthy flavor. Here it is enhanced by a quick soak in a soy-based marinade. Sweet peanut sauce and corn fritters balance the tempeh's savory flavor.

DAIRY-FREE,
VEGETARIAN

Prep time: 15 minutes, plus 15 minutes to marinate
Cook time: 15 minutes

FOR THE TEMPEH

1 (8-ounce) package tempeh

3 tablespoons fresh lemon juice, divided

2 tablespoons soy sauce, divided

2 garlic cloves, chopped

½ teaspoon ground turmeric

2 tablespoons vegetable oil

¾ cup canned full-fat coconut milk

4 tablespoons peanut butter

1 teaspoon light brown sugar

½ teaspoon red pepper flakes

1 scallion, chopped

FOR THE CORN FRITTERS

2 cups frozen corn, thawed and drained

2 scallions, thinly sliced

¼ cup chopped fresh cilantro

¼ teaspoon kosher salt

2 large eggs

½ cup all-purpose flour

2 tablespoons vegetable oil

1. **To prep the tempeh:** Slice the tempeh into ¼-inch-thick slabs.

2. In a large bowl, combine 2 tablespoons of lemon juice, 1 tablespoon of soy sauce, the garlic, turmeric, and oil.

3. Add the tempeh to the marinade and toss to coat the pieces. Let marinate for 15 minutes.

4. In a medium bowl, whisk together the coconut milk, peanut butter, remaining 1 tablespoon of lemon juice, remaining 1 tablespoon of soy sauce, brown sugar, red pepper flakes, and scallion. Set aside.

5. To prep the corn fritters: In a large bowl, combine the corn, scallions, cilantro, and salt. Mix in the eggs and flour until everything is well combined.

6. To cook the tempeh and fritters: Install a broil rack in the Zone 1 basket. Arrange the tempeh in a single layer on the rack and insert the basket in the unit. Install a crisper plate in the Zone 2 basket. Spoon 2 tablespoons of corn fritter batter into each corner of the basket and drizzle with oil. Flatten slightly with the back of the spoon and insert the basket in the unit.

7. Select Zone 1, select AIR BROIL, set the temperature to 400°F, and set the timer to 8 minutes.

8. Select Zone 2, select AIR FRY, set the temperature to 375°F, and set the timer to 15 minutes. Select SMART FINISH.™

9. Press START/PAUSE to begin cooking.

10. When the Zone 2 timer reads 5 minutes, press START/PAUSE. Remove the basket and use silicone-tipped tongs or a spatula to flip the corn fritters. Reinsert the basket and press START/PAUSE to resume cooking.

11. When cooking is complete, the tempeh will be golden brown and the corn fritters set in the center and browned on the edges.

12. Serve the tempeh with the peanut sauce for dipping and the corn fritters on the side.

Per serving: Calories: 578; Total fat: 40g; Saturated fat: 14g; Carbohydrates: 39g; Fiber: 3.5g; Protein: 24g; Sodium: 815mg

Super swap: Pair the tempeh and satay sauce with Baked Brown Sugar Acorn Squash (page 139) or Green Salad with Baked Croutons (page 182), replacing the crispy fried goat cheese with the tempeh.

Green Salad with Crispy Fried Goat Cheese and Baked Croutons

SERVES 4

These baked croutons are one of my favorite things to make in my Ninja® Foodi® Air Fryer. They're so easy to make and come out so crunchy! Store-bought croutons can't even begin to compare. To make this salad extra special, I added crispy air-fried goat cheese rounds. Each round is both melty and crisp, making every bite a delicious contrast of textures.

NUT-FREE, VEGETARIAN

Prep time: 10 minutes, plus 5 minutes to cool
Cook time: 10 minutes

FOR THE GOAT CHEESE
1 (4-ounce) log soft goat cheese

½ cup panko bread crumbs

2 tablespoons vegetable oil

FOR THE CROUTONS
2 slices Italian-style sandwich bread

2 tablespoons vegetable oil

1 tablespoon poultry seasoning

½ teaspoon kosher salt

¼ teaspoon freshly ground black pepper

FOR THE SALAD
8 cups green leaf lettuce leaves

½ cup store-bought balsamic vinaigrette

1. **To prep the goat cheese:** Cut the goat cheese into 8 round slices.

2. Spread the panko on a plate. Gently press the cheese into the panko to coat on both sides. Drizzle with the oil.

3. **To prep the croutons:** Cut the bread into cubes and place them in a large bowl. Add the oil, poultry seasoning, salt, and black pepper. Mix well to coat the bread cubes evenly.

4. **To cook the goat cheese and croutons:** Install a crisper plate in each of the two baskets. Place the goat cheese in the Zone 1 basket and insert the basket in the unit. Place the croutons in the Zone 2 basket and insert the basket in the unit.

5. Select Zone 1, select AIR FRY, set the temperature to 400ºF, and set the timer to 6 minutes.

6. Select Zone 2, select BAKE, set the temperature to 390ºF, and set the timer to 10 minutes. Select SMART FINISH.™

7. Press START/PAUSE to begin cooking.

8. When cooking is complete, the goat cheese will be golden brown and the croutons crisp.

9. Remove the Zone 1 basket. Let the goat cheese cool in the basket for 5 minutes; it will firm up as it cools.

10. To assemble the salad: In a large bowl, combine the lettuce, vinaigrette, and croutons. Toss well. Divide the salad among four plates. Top each plate with 2 pieces of goat cheese.

Per serving: Calories: 578; Total fat: 40g; Saturated fat: 14g; Carbohydrates: 39g; Fiber: 3.5g; Protein: 24g; Sodium: 815mg

Super swap: Skip the croutons on this salad and top it with Crispy Chickpeas (page 66) or add these croutons to the Roasted Vegetable Salad (page 98).

Caprese Panini with Zucchini Chips

SERVES 4

Nothing beats a nice, gooey panini, and this is one of the best. It's stuffed with creamy mozzarella, juicy tomatoes, and vibrant pesto—and air-frying them makes the bread so crispy! I've paired these tasty sandwiches with crisp zucchini "chips" coated in seasoned bread crumbs and salty Parmesan. Enjoy them plain or dunk them in your favorite marinara sauce.

VEGETARIAN

Prep time: 20 minutes
Cook time: 20 minutes

FOR THE PANINI

4 tablespoons pesto

8 slices Italian-style sandwich bread

1 tomato, diced

6 ounces fresh mozzarella cheese, shredded

¼ cup mayonnaise

FOR THE ZUCCHINI CHIPS

½ cup all-purpose flour

2 large eggs

¼ teaspoon freshly ground black pepper

⅛ teaspoon kosher salt

½ cup panko bread crumbs

¼ cup grated Parmesan cheese

1 teaspoon Italian seasoning

1 medium zucchini, cut into ¼-inch-thick rounds

2 tablespoons vegetable oil

1. To prep the panini: Spread 1 tablespoon of pesto each on 4 slices of the bread. Layer the diced tomato and shredded mozzarella on the other 4 slices of bread. Top the tomato/cheese mixture with the pesto-coated bread, pesto-side down, to form 4 sandwiches.

2. Spread the outside of each sandwich (both bread slices) with a thin layer of the mayonnaise.

3. To prep the zucchini chips: Set up a breading station with three small shallow bowls. Place the flour in the first bowl. In the second bowl, beat together the eggs, salt, and black pepper. Place the panko, Parmesan, and Italian seasoning in the third bowl.

4. Bread the zucchini in this order: First, dip the slices into the flour, coating both sides. Then, dip into the beaten egg. Finally, coat in the panko mixture. Drizzle the zucchini on both sides with the oil.

5. To cook the panini and zucchini chips: Install a crisper plate in each of the two baskets. Place 2 sandwiches in the Zone 1 basket and insert the basket in the unit. Place half of the zucchini chips in a single layer in the Zone 2 basket and insert the basket in the unit.

6. Select Zone 1, select AIR FRY, set the temperature to 375°F, and set the timer to 20 minutes.

7. Select Zone 2, select AIR FRY, set the temperature to 400°F, and set the timer to 20 minutes. Select SMART FINISH.™

8. Press START/PAUSE to begin cooking.

9. When the Zone 1 timer reads 15 minutes, press START/PAUSE. Remove the basket, and use silicone-tipped tongs or a spatula to flip the sandwiches. Reinsert the basket and press START/PAUSE to resume cooking.

10. When both timers read 10 minutes, press START/PAUSE. Remove the Zone 1 basket and transfer the sandwiches to a plate. Place the remaining 2 sandwiches into the basket and insert the basket in the unit. Remove the Zone 2 basket and transfer the zucchini chips to a serving plate. Place the remaining zucchini chips in the basket. Reinsert the basket and press START/PAUSE to resume cooking.

CONTINUED >

Caprese Panini with Zucchini Chips continued

Super swap: Serve these panini with Barbecue Potato Chips (page 114), Cauliflower "Wings" (page 89), or Seasoned Potato Wedges (page 155).

11. When the Zone 1 timer reads 5 minutes, press START/PAUSE. Remove the basket and flip the sandwiches. Reinsert the basket and press START/PAUSE to resume cooking.

12. When cooking is complete, the panini should be toasted and the zucchini chips golden brown and crisp.

13. Cut each panini in half. Serve hot with zucchini chips on the side.

Per serving: *Calories: 751; Total fat: 39g; Saturated fat: 9.5g; Carbohydrates: 77g; Fiber: 3.5g; Protein: 23g; Sodium: 1,086mg*

Buffalo Seitan with Crispy Zucchini Noodles

SERVES 4

I can't get enough of these crispy, tempura-battered zucchini noodles. Sometimes I make them just to snack on! Be sure to use fresh zucchini noodles since frozen ones won't crisp in the air fryer. Prepared seitan is an easy add-on for a simple vegetarian dinner. Here, I've coated it in spicy wing-style sauce to pair with the milder zucchini. If you like your sauce milder, you can add melted butter to mellow it out; or for an even spicier sauce, mix in a pinch of cayenne with the other sauce ingredients.

DAIRY-FREE, NUT-FREE, VEGETARIAN

Prep time: 15 minutes
Cook time: 12 minutes

FOR THE BUFFALO SEITAN

- 1 (8-ounce) package precooked seitan strips
- 1 teaspoon garlic powder, divided
- ½ teaspoon onion powder
- ¼ teaspoon smoked paprika
- ¼ cup Louisiana-style hot sauce
- 2 tablespoons vegetable oil
- 1 tablespoon tomato paste
- ¼ teaspoon freshly ground black pepper

FOR THE ZUCCHINI NOODLES

- 3 large egg whites
- 1¼ cups all-purpose flour
- 1 teaspoon kosher salt, divided
- 12 ounces seltzer water or club soda
- 5 ounces zucchini noodles
- Nonstick cooking spray

1. **To prep the Buffalo seitan:** Season the seitan strips with ½ teaspoon of garlic powder, the onion powder, and smoked paprika.

2. In a large bowl, whisk together the hot sauce, oil, tomato paste, remaining ½ teaspoon of garlic powder, and the black pepper. Set the bowl of Buffalo sauce aside.

3. **To prep the zucchini noodles:** In a medium bowl, use a handheld mixer to beat the egg whites until stiff peaks form.

CONTINUED >

Variation: Substitute ½ cup of your favorite barbecue sauce for the wing sauce.

Super swap: Buffalo seitan is also delicious with "Fried" Onion Rings (page 189) or Mexican Rice (page 116). Try the Crispy Zucchini Noodles with Balsamic-Glazed Tofu (page 178) or Italian-Style Meatballs (page 108).

4. In a large bowl, combine the flour and ½ teaspoon of salt. Mix in the seltzer to form a thin batter. Fold in the beaten egg whites.

5. Add the zucchini to the batter and gently mix to coat.

6. To cook the seitan and zucchini noodles: Install a crisper plate in each of the two baskets. Place the seitan in the Zone 1 basket and insert the basket in the unit. Lift the noodles from the batter one at a time, letting the excess drip off, and place them in the Zone 2 basket. Insert the basket in the unit.

7. Select Zone 1, select BAKE, set the temperature to 370°F, and set the timer to 12 minutes.

8. Select Zone 2, select AIR FRY, set the temperature to 400°F, and set the timer to 12 minutes. Select SMART FINISH.™

9. Press START/PAUSE to begin cooking.

10. When the Zone 1 timer reads 2 minutes, press START/PAUSE. Remove the basket and transfer the seitan to the bowl of Buffalo sauce. Turn to coat, then return the seitan to the basket. Reinsert the basket and press START/PAUSE to resume cooking.

11. When cooking is complete, the seitan should be warmed through and the zucchini noodles crisp and light golden brown.

12. Sprinkle the zucchini noodles with the remaining ½ teaspoon of salt. If desired, drizzle extra Buffalo sauce over the seitan. Serve hot.

Per serving: Calories: 252; Total fat: 15g; Saturated fat: 1g; Carbohydrates: 22g; Fiber: 1.5g; Protein: 13g; Sodium: 740mg

Veggie Burgers with "Fried" Onion Rings

SERVES 4

You won't believe how easy it is to make your own veggie burgers from scratch. These are so much tastier than store-bought and you'll feel great about knowing exactly what's in them. I like pairing these with barbecue sauce and crispy onion rings. For a real treat, slip an onion ring or two on the burger.

DAIRY-FREE, NUT-FREE, VEGETARIAN

Prep time: 20 minutes
Cook time: 25 minutes

Per serving: *Calories: 538; Total fat: 16g; Saturated fat: 2g; Carbohydrates: 83g; Fiber: 10g; Protein: 19g; Sodium: 914mg*

FOR THE VEGGIE BURGERS

1 (15-ounce) can black beans, drained and rinsed

½ cup panko bread crumbs

1 large egg

¼ cup finely chopped red bell pepper

¼ cup frozen corn, thawed

1 tablespoon olive oil

½ teaspoon garlic powder

½ teaspoon ground cumin

¼ teaspoon smoked paprika

Nonstick cooking spray

4 hamburger buns

¼ cup barbecue sauce, for serving

FOR THE ONION RINGS

1 large sweet onion

½ cup all-purpose flour

2 large eggs

1 cup panko bread crumbs

½ teaspoon kosher salt

Nonstick cooking spray

1. **To prep the veggie burgers:** In a large bowl, mash the beans with a potato masher or a fork. Stir in the panko, egg, bell pepper, corn, oil, garlic powder, cumin, and smoked paprika. Mix well.

2. Shape the mixture into 4 patties. Spritz both sides of each patty with cooking spray.

3. **To prep the onion rings:** Cut the onion into ½-inch-thick rings.

4. Set up a breading station with three small shallow bowls. Place the flour in the first bowl. In the second bowl, beat the eggs. Place the panko and salt in the third bowl.

Veggie Burgers with "Fried" Onion Rings continued

Super swap: These burgers are also great with Sweet Potato Fries (page 157), Warm Baked Potato Salad (page 93), or Street Corn (page 76).

5. Bread the onions rings in this order: First, dip them into the flour, coating both sides. Then, dip into the beaten egg. Finally, coat them in the panko. Spritz each with cooking spray.

6. To cook the burgers and onion rings: Install a crisper plate in each of the two baskets. Place 2 veggie burgers in the Zone 1 basket. Place the onion rings in the Zone 2 basket and insert both baskets in the unit.

7. Select Zone 1, select AIR FRY, set the temperature to 390°F, and set the timer to 25 minutes.

8. Select Zone 2, select AIR FRY, set the temperature to 375°F, and set the timer to 10 minutes. Select SMART FINISH.™

9. Press START/PAUSE to begin cooking.

10. When the Zone 1 timer reads 10 minutes, press START/PAUSE. Remove the basket and use a silicone spatula to flip the burgers. Reinsert the basket and press START/PAUSE to resume cooking.

11. When the Zone 1 timer reads 10 minutes, press START/PAUSE. Remove the basket and transfer the burgers to a plate. Place the 2 remaining burgers in the basket. Reinsert the basket and press START/PAUSE to resume cooking.

12. When both timers read 5 minutes, press START/PAUSE. Remove the Zone 1 basket and flip the burgers, then reinsert the basket. Remove the Zone 2 basket and shake vigorously to rearrange the onion rings and separate any that have stuck together. Reinsert the basket and press START/PAUSE to resume cooking.

13. When cooking is complete, the veggie burgers should be cooked through and the onion rings golden brown.

14. Place 1 burger on each bun. Top with barbecue sauce and serve with onion rings on the side.

Walnut Baklava Bites // Pistachio Baklava Bites, *page 202*

8

Desserts

Apple Crumble // Peach Crumble

SERVES 8

If you ask me, two desserts are always better than one. This recipe takes advantage of the Ninja® Foodi® 2-Basket Air Fryer's dual drawers to make two variations on a classic fruit crumble. With an apple-cinnamon crumble in one side and a juicy peach crumble in the other, you'll be in dessert heaven within minutes.

DAIRY-FREE, NUT-FREE, VEGETARIAN

Prep time: 15 minutes
Cook time: 20 minutes

FOR THE APPLE CRUMBLE

½ cup packed light brown sugar

¼ cup all-purpose flour

¼ cup rolled oats

2 tablespoons unsalted butter, at room temperature

½ teaspoon ground cinnamon

¼ teaspoon ground nutmeg

⅛ teaspoon kosher salt

4 medium Granny Smith apples, sliced

FOR THE PEACH CRUMBLE

½ cup packed light brown sugar

¼ cup all-purpose flour

¼ cup rolled oats

2 tablespoons unsalted butter, at room temperature

½ teaspoon ground cinnamon

⅛ teaspoon kosher salt

4 peaches, peeled and sliced

1. **To prep the apple crumble:** In a medium bowl, combine the brown sugar, flour, oats, butter, cinnamon, nutmeg, and salt and mix well. The mixture will be dry and crumbly.

2. **To prep the peach crumble:** In a medium bowl, combine the brown sugar, flour, oats, butter, cinnamon, and salt and mix well. The mixture will be dry and crumbly.

3. To cook both crumbles: Spread the apples in the Zone 1 basket in an even layer. Top evenly with the apple crumble topping and insert the basket in the unit. Spread the peaches in the Zone 2 basket in an even layer. Top with the peach crumble topping and insert the basket in the unit.

4. Select Zone 1, select BAKE, set the temperature to 350ºF, and set the timer to 20 minutes. Select MATCH COOK™ to match Zone 2 settings to Zone 1.

5. Press START/PAUSE to begin cooking.

6. When cooking is complete, the fruit will be tender and the crumble topping crisp and golden brown. Serve warm or at room temperature.

Per serving (apple): Calories: 300; Total fat: 6.5g; Saturated fat: 3.5g; Carbohydrates: 59g; Fiber: 5.5g; Protein: 2g; Sodium: 45mg

Per serving (peach): Calories: 261; Total fat: 6.5g; Saturated fat: 3.5g; Carbohydrates: 51g; Fiber: 3g; Protein: 3g; Sodium: 44mg

Variation: Use your favorite canned pie filling instead of the fresh fruit. I love cherry!

Banana Spring Rolls with Hot Fudge Dip

SERVES 4

These crispy rolls are filled with sweet bananas and air-fried until golden brown. I love how the crisp wrapper contrasts with the soft banana center, but the real star of this dessert is the rich and gooey hot fudge dip.

NUT-FREE, VEGETARIAN

Prep time: 10 minutes, plus 3 minutes to cool
Cook time: 10 minutes

FOR THE BANANA SPRING ROLLS
1 large banana
4 egg roll wrappers
4 teaspoons light brown sugar
Nonstick cooking spray

FOR THE HOT FUDGE DIP
¼ cup sweetened condensed milk
2 tablespoons semisweet chocolate chips
1 tablespoon unsweetened cocoa powder
1 tablespoon unsalted butter
⅛ teaspoon kosher salt
⅛ teaspoon vanilla extract

1. **To prep the banana spring rolls:** Peel the banana and halve it crosswise. Cut each piece in half lengthwise, for a total of 4 pieces.

2. Place one piece of banana diagonally across an egg roll wrapper. Sprinkle with 1 teaspoon of brown sugar. Fold the edges of the egg roll wrapper over the ends of the banana, then roll to enclose the banana inside. Brush the edge of the wrapper with water and press to seal. Spritz with cooking spray. Repeat with the remaining bananas, egg roll wrappers, and brown sugar.

3. **To prep the hot fudge dip:** In an ovenproof ramekin or bowl, combine the condensed milk, chocolate chips, cocoa powder, butter, salt, and vanilla.

4. To cook the spring rolls and hot fudge dip: Install a crisper plate in each of the two baskets. Place the banana spring rolls seam-side down in the Zone 1 basket and insert the basket in the unit. Place the ramekin in the Zone 2 basket and insert the basket in the unit.

5. Select Zone 1, select AIR FRY, set the temperature to 390ºF, and set the timer to 10 minutes.

6. Select Zone 2, select BAKE, set the temperature to 330ºF, and set the timer to 8 minutes. Select SMART FINISH.™

7. Press START/PAUSE to begin cooking.

8. When the Zone 2 timer reads 3 minutes, press START/PAUSE. Remove the basket and stir the hot fudge until smooth. Reinsert the basket and press START/PAUSE to resume cooking.

9. When cooking is complete, the spring rolls should be crisp.

10. Let the hot fudge cool for 2 to 3 minutes. Serve the banana spring rolls with hot fudge for dipping.

Variation: Add ½ teaspoon of cinnamon and a pinch of cayenne pepper to the hot fudge for a Mexican-inspired dip.

Per serving: Calories: 268; Total fat: 10g; Saturated fat: 4g; Carbohydrates: 42g; Fiber: 2g; Protein: 5g; Sodium: 245mg

Cinnamon-Sugar "Churros" with Caramel Sauce

SERVES 4

Churros are traditionally made with a cooked pastry dough, similar to the pâte à choux that you'd use to make éclairs. Since it can be a little finicky, I've simplified things by using store-bought puff pastry instead. The texture is a little lighter and crisper, but it has that same cinnamon-sugar flavor you know and love—especially when dipped in sticky caramel sauce.

NUT-FREE, VEGETARIAN

Prep time: 5 minutes, plus 10 minutes to cool
Cook time: 10 minutes

FOR THE "CHURROS"
1 sheet frozen puff pastry, thawed

Butter-flavored cooking spray

1 tablespoon granulated sugar

1 teaspoon ground cinnamon

FOR THE CARAMEL SAUCE
½ cup packed light brown sugar

2 tablespoons unsalted butter, cut into small pieces

¼ cup heavy (whipping) cream

2 teaspoons vanilla extract

⅛ teaspoon kosher salt

1. **To prep the "churros":** Cut the puff pastry crosswise into 4 rectangles. Fold each piece in half lengthwise to make a long thin "churro."

2. **To prep the caramel sauce:** Measure the brown sugar, butter, cream, and vanilla into an ovenproof ramekin or bowl (no need to stir).

3. **To cook the "churros" and caramel sauce:** Install a crisper plate in the Zone 1 basket. Place the "churros" in the basket and insert the basket in the unit. Place the ramekin in the Zone 2 basket and insert the basket in the unit.

4. Select Zone 1, select AIR FRY, set the temperature to 330°F, and set the timer to 10 minutes.

5. Select Zone 2, select BAKE, set the temperature to 350ºF, and set the timer to 10 minutes. Select SMART FINISH.™

6. Press START/PAUSE to begin cooking.

7. When the Zone 2 timer reads 5 minutes, press START/PAUSE. Remove the basket and stir the caramel. Reinsert the basket and press START/PAUSE to resume cooking.

8. When cooking is complete, the "churros" will be golden brown and cooked through and the caramel sauce smooth.

9. Spritz each "churro" with cooking spray and sprinkle generously with the granulated sugar and cinnamon.

10. Stir the salt into the caramel sauce. Let cool for 5 to 10 minutes before serving. Note that the caramel will thicken as it cools.

Per serving: *Calories: 460; Total fat: 26g; Saturated fat: 14g; Carbohydrates: 60g; Fiber: 1.5g; Protein: 5g; Sodium: 254mg*

S'mores Dip with Cinnamon-Sugar Tortillas

SERVES 4

This sweet dip was inspired by the dessert my husband and I shared after our last anniversary dinner. It was the perfect end to the meal and a clever way to enjoy s'mores all year long. Dip, dunk, and enjoy!

VEGETARIAN

Prep time: 5 minutes, plus 3 minutes to cool
Cook time: 5 minutes

FOR THE S'MORES DIP

½ **cup chocolate-hazelnut spread**

¼ **cup milk chocolate or white chocolate chips**

¼ **cup graham cracker crumbs**

½ **cup mini marshmallows**

FOR THE CINNAMON-SUGAR TORTILLAS

4 **(6-inch) flour tortillas**

Butter-flavored cooking spray

1 **teaspoon granulated sugar**

½ **teaspoon ground cinnamon**

¼ **teaspoon ground cardamom (optional)**

1. **To prep the s'mores dip:** Spread the chocolate-hazelnut spread in the bottom of a shallow ovenproof ramekin or dish.

2. Scatter the chocolate chips and graham cracker crumbs over the top. Arrange the marshmallows in a single layer on top of the crumbs.

3. **To prep the tortillas:** Spray both sides of each tortilla with cooking spray. Cut each tortilla into 8 wedges and sprinkle both sides evenly with sugar, cinnamon, and cardamom (if using).

4. **To cook the dip and tortillas:** Install a crisper plate in each of the two baskets. Place the ramekin in the Zone 1 basket and insert the basket in the unit. Place the tortillas in the Zone 2 basket and insert the basket in the unit.

5. Select Zone 1, select BAKE, set the temperature to 330°F, and set the timer to 5 minutes.

6. Select Zone 2, select AIR FRY, set the temperature to 375ºF, and set the timer to 5 minutes. Select SMART FINISH.™

7. Press START/PAUSE to begin cooking.

8. When the Zone 2 timer reads 3 minutes, press START/PAUSE. Remove the basket and shake it to redistribute the chips. Reinsert the basket and press START/PAUSE to resume cooking.

9. When cooking is complete, the dip will be bubbling and golden brown and the chips crispy.

10. If desired, toast the marshmallows more: Select Zone 1, select AIR BROIL, set the temperature to 450ºF, and set the timer to 1 minute. Cook until the marshmallows are deep golden brown.

11. Let the dip cool for 2 to 3 minutes. Serve with the cinnamon-sugar tortilla chips.

Per serving: *Calories: 404; Total fat: 18g; Saturated fat: 7g; Carbohydrates: 54g; Fiber: 2.5g; Protein: 6g; Sodium: 346mg*

Walnut Baklava Bites //
Pistachio Baklava Bites

MAKES 12 BAKLAVA BITES

This baklava is an easy, simplified version of the classic. The flaky phyllo dough pastry is filled with a simple walnut or pistachio filling that comes together in just minutes. They're both delicious options, and I can never decide which one I like better!

VEGETARIAN

Prep time: 10 minutes, plus 1 hour to cool
Cook time: 10 minutes

FOR THE WALNUT BAKLAVA BITES

¼ cup finely chopped walnuts

2 teaspoons cold unsalted butter, grated

2 teaspoons granulated sugar

½ teaspoon ground cinnamon

6 frozen phyllo shells (from a 1.9-ounce package), thawed

FOR THE PISTACHIO BAKLAVA BITES

¼ cup finely chopped pistachios

2 teaspoons very cold unsalted butter, grated

2 teaspoons granulated sugar

¼ teaspoon ground cardamom (optional)

6 frozen phyllo shells (from a 1.9-ounce package), thawed

FOR THE HONEY SYRUP

¼ cup hot water

¼ cup honey

2 teaspoons fresh lemon juice

1. **To prep the walnut baklava bites:** In a small bowl, combine the walnuts, butter, sugar, and cinnamon. Spoon the filling into the phyllo shells.

2. **To prep the pistachio baklava bites:** In a small bowl, combine the pistachios, butter, sugar, and cardamom (if using). Spoon the filling into the phyllo shells.

3. **To cook the baklava bites:** Install a crisper plate in each of the two baskets. Place the walnut baklava bites in the Zone 1 basket and insert the basket in the unit. Place the pistachio baklava bites in the Zone 2 basket and insert the basket in the unit.

4. Select Zone 1, select BAKE, set the temperature to 330°F, and set the timer to 10 minutes. Press MATCH COOK™ to match Zone 2 settings to Zone 1.

5. Press START/PAUSE to begin cooking.

6. When cooking is complete, the shells will be golden brown and crisp.

7. **To make the honey syrup:** In a small bowl, whisk together the hot water, honey, and lemon juice. Dividing evenly, pour the syrup over the baklava bites (you may hear a crackling sound).

8. Let cool completely before serving, about 1 hour.

Per serving (3 walnut baklava bites): *Calories: 262; Total fat: 16g; Saturated fat: 3g; Carbohydrates: 29g; Fiber: 1g; Protein: 2g; Sodium: 39mg*

Per serving (3 pistachio baklava bites): *Calories: 236; Total fat: 12g; Saturated fat: 3g; Carbohydrates: 31g; Fiber: 1.5g; Protein: 3g; Sodium: 39mg*

Prep tip: Phyllo shells are preshaped and ready to go, so you don't need to spend time rolling and stacking individual sheets of phyllo. Look for them in the freezer case of your grocery store.

Lemon Sugar Cookie Bars //
Monster Sugar Cookie Bars

MAKES 12 COOKIE BARS

These soft and chewy sugar cookie bars deliver big flavor. The lemon version is tart and refreshing while the monster cookies are stuffed with chocolate candies, oats, and peanut butter chips. Making bars instead of individual cookies helps maximize space in the air fryer, so you don't need to make back-to-back batches. Pick your favorite version and serve it with a big glass of cold milk.

VEGETARIAN

Prep time: 15 minutes, plus
1 hour to cool
Cook time: 18 minutes

FOR THE LEMON COOKIE BARS

**Grated zest and juice
of 1 lemon**

½ cup granulated sugar

**4 tablespoons (½ stick)
unsalted butter, at
room temperature**

1 large egg yolk

1 teaspoon vanilla extract

⅛ teaspoon baking powder

**½ cup plus 2 tablespoons
all-purpose flour**

FOR THE MONSTER COOKIE BARS

½ cup granulated sugar

**4 tablespoons (½ stick)
unsalted butter, at
room temperature**

1 large egg yolk

1 teaspoon vanilla extract

⅛ teaspoon baking powder

**½ cup plus 2 tablespoons
all-purpose flour**

¼ cup rolled oats

¼ cup M&M's

¼ cup peanut butter chips

1. **To prep the lemon cookie bars:** In a large bowl, rub together the lemon zest and sugar. Add the butter and use a hand mixer to beat until light and fluffy.

2. Beat in the egg yolk, vanilla, and lemon juice. Mix in the baking powder and flour.

3. **To prep the monster cookie bars:** In a large bowl, with a hand mixer, beat the sugar and butter until light and fluffy.

4. Beat in the egg yolk and vanilla. Mix in the baking powder and flour. Stir in the oats, M&M's, and peanut butter chips.

5. To cook the cookie bars: Line both baskets with aluminum foil. Press the lemon cookie dough into the Zone 1 basket and insert the basket in the unit. Press the monster cookie dough into the Zone 2 basket and insert the basket in the unit.

6. Select Zone 1, select BAKE, set the temperature to 330°F, and set the timer to 18 minutes. Press MATCH COOK™ to match Zone 2 settings to Zone 1.

7. Press START/PAUSE to begin cooking.

8. When cooking is complete, the cookies should be set in the middle and have begun to pull away from the sides of the basket.

9. Let the cookies cool completely, about 1 hour. Cut each basket into 6 bars for a total of 12 bars.

Per serving (1 lemon cookie bar): *Calories: 191; Total fat: 8.5g; Saturated fat: 5g; Carbohydrates: 27g; Fiber: 0.5g; Protein: 2g; Sodium: 3mg*

Per serving (1 monster cookie bar): *Calories: 271; Total fat: 12g; Saturated fat: 7g; Carbohydrates: 38g; Fiber: 1g; Protein: 3g; Sodium: 20mg*

Variation: For even more sweet and salty flavor, add chopped pretzels or potato chips to the monster cookies instead of the peanut butter chips.

Fried Dough with Roasted Strawberries

SERVES 4

This fried dough reminds me of the ones I would always get at the fair when I was a kid. It's so light and crispy on the outside, but warm and doughy in the middle. Dust it with powdered sugar and top it with sweetened roasted strawberries for a delicious treat your whole family will love.

DAIRY-FREE, NUT-FREE, VEGAN

Prep time: 5 minutes
Cook time: 20 minutes

FOR THE FRIED DOUGH

6 ounces refrigerated pizza dough, at room temperature

2 tablespoons all-purpose flour, for dusting

4 tablespoons vegetable oil

2 tablespoons powdered sugar

FOR THE ROASTED STRAWBERRIES

2 cups frozen whole strawberries

2 tablespoons granulated sugar

1. **To prep the fried dough:** Divide the dough into four equal portions.

2. Dust a clean work surface with the flour. Place one dough portion on the surface and use a rolling pin to roll to a ⅛-inch thickness. Rub both sides of the dough with 1 tablespoon of oil. Repeat with remaining dough portions and oil.

3. **To prep the strawberries:** Place the strawberries in the Zone 2 basket. Sprinkle the granulated sugar on top.

4. **To cook the fried dough and strawberries:** Install a crisper plate in the Zone 1 basket. Place 2 dough portions in the basket and insert the basket in the unit. Insert the Zone 2 basket in the unit.

5. Select Zone 1, select AIR FRY, set the temperature to 400°F, and set the timer to 18 minutes.

CONTINUED >

Fried Dough with Roasted Strawberries continued

Variation: Swap the strawberries for frozen blueberries.

6. Select Zone 2, select ROAST, set the temperature to 330ºF, and set the timer to 20 minutes. Select SMART FINISH.™

7. Press START/PAUSE to begin cooking.

8. When both timers read 8 minutes, press START/PAUSE. Remove the Zone 1 basket and transfer the fried dough to a cutting board. Place the 2 remaining dough portions in the basket, then reinsert the basket. Remove the Zone 2 basket and stir the strawberries. Reinsert the basket and press START/PAUSE to resume cooking.

9. When cooking is complete, the dough should be cooked through and the strawberries soft and jammy.

10. Sprinkle the fried dough with powdered sugar. Gently mash the strawberries with a fork. Spoon the strawberries onto each fried dough portion and serve.

Per serving: *Calories: 304; Total fat: 15g; Saturated fat: 2.5g; Carbohydrates: 38g; Fiber: 0.5g; Protein: 3g; Sodium: 421mg*

Pumpkin Hand Pies // Blueberry Hand Pies

MAKES 4 HAND PIES

These mini pies are seriously scrumptious! Whether you reach for the classic pumpkin pie or the fresh blueberry version, you'll love having homemade pies at your fingertips! Air-frying these pies instead of baking them makes the crusts extra crisp and flaky.

NUT-FREE, VEGETARIAN

Prep time: 15 minutes, plus 30 minutes to cool
Cook time: 15 minutes

FOR THE PUMPKIN HAND PIES

½ cup pumpkin pie filling (from a 15-ounce can)

⅓ cup half-and-half

1 large egg

½ refrigerated pie crust (from a 14.1-ounce package)

1 large egg yolk

1 tablespoon whole milk

FOR THE BLUEBERRY HAND PIES

¼ cup blueberries

2 tablespoons granulated sugar

1 tablespoon grated lemon zest (optional)

¼ teaspoon cornstarch

1 teaspoon fresh lemon juice

⅛ teaspoon kosher salt

½ refrigerated pie crust (from a 14.1-ounce package)

1 large egg yolk

1 tablespoon whole milk

½ teaspoon turbinado sugar

1. **To prep the pumpkin hand pies:** In a small bowl, mix the pumpkin pie filling, half-and-half, and whole egg until well combined and smooth.

2. Cut the dough in half to form two wedges. Divide the pumpkin pie filling between the wedges. Fold the crust over to completely encase the filling. Using a fork, crimp the edges, forming a tight seal.

3. In a small bowl, whisk together the egg yolk and milk. Brush over the pastry. Carefully cut two small vents in the top of each pie.

CONTINUED >

4. To prep the blueberry hand pies: In a small bowl, combine the blueberries, granulated sugar, lemon zest (if using), cornstarch, lemon juice, and salt.

5. Cut the dough in half to form two wedges. Divide the blueberry filling between the wedges. Fold the crust over to completely encase the filling. Using a fork, crimp the edges, forming a tight seal.

6. In a small bowl, whisk together the egg yolk and milk. Brush over the pastry. Sprinkle with the turbinado sugar. Carefully cut two small vents in the top of each pie.

7. To cook the hand pies: Install a crisper plate in each of the two baskets. Place the pumpkin hand pies in the Zone 1 basket and insert the basket in the unit. Place the blueberry hand pies in the Zone 2 basket and insert the basket in the unit.

8. Select Zone 1, select AIR FRY, set the temperature to 350°F, and set the timer to 15 minutes. Select MATCH COOK™ to match Zone 2 settings to Zone 1.

9. Press START/PAUSE to begin cooking.

10. When cooking is complete, the pie crust should be crisp and golden brown and the filling bubbling.

11. Let the hand pies cool for at least 30 minutes before serving.

Per serving (1 pumpkin hand pie): *Calories: 588; Total fat: 33g; Saturated fat: 14g; Carbohydrates: 68g; Fiber: 0.5g; Protein: 10g; Sodium: 583mg*

Per serving (1 blueberry hand pie): *Calories: 494; Total fat: 26g; Saturated fat: 11g; Carbohydrates: 65g; Fiber: 0.5g; Protein: 6g; Sodium: 594mg*

"Air-Fried" Oreos // Apple Fries

SERVES 4

I was thrilled when I discovered that I could make "deep-fried" Oreos in my Ninja® Foodi® Air Fryer! The batter is quick to prepare and cooks up light and cakey, with a crisp, golden exterior. I love throwing a few apples into the same batter for apple fries. The contrast of sweet dough and tart fruit is so good. Dusting the apples with cornstarch helps keep the batter from slipping off as it cooks.

NUT-FREE, VEGETARIAN

Prep time: 15 minutes
Cook time: 10 minutes

Per serving (1 Oreo):
Calories: 464; Total fat: 21g;
Saturated fat: 3.5g;
Carbohydrates: 66g; Fiber: 2.5g;
Protein: 7g; Sodium: 293mg

Per serving (half of the apple
fries): Calories: 476; Total fat: 28g;
Saturated fat: 1g;
Carbohydrates: 62g; Fiber: 5.5g;
Protein: 7g; Sodium: 115mg

FOR THE "FRIED" OREOS
- 1 teaspoon vegetable oil
- 1 cup all-purpose flour
- 1 tablespoon granulated sugar
- 1 tablespoon baking powder
- ½ teaspoon baking soda
- ¼ teaspoon kosher salt
- 1 large egg
- ¼ cup unsweetened almond milk
- ½ teaspoon vanilla extract
- 8 Oreo cookies
- Nonstick cooking spray
- 1 tablespoon powdered sugar (optional)

FOR THE APPLE FRIES
- 1 teaspoon vegetable oil
- 1 cup all-purpose flour
- 1 tablespoon granulated sugar
- 1 tablespoon baking powder
- ½ teaspoon baking soda
- ¼ teaspoon kosher salt
- 1 large egg
- ¼ cup unsweetened almond milk
- ½ teaspoon vanilla extract
- 2 Granny Smith apples
- 2 tablespoons cornstarch
- ½ teaspoon apple pie spice
- Nonstick cooking spray
- 1 tablespoon powdered sugar (optional)

1. **To prep the "fried" Oreos:** Brush a crisper plate with the oil and install it in the Zone 1 basket.

2. In a large bowl, combine the flour, granulated sugar, baking powder, baking soda, and salt. Mix in the egg, almond milk, and vanilla to form a thick batter.

3. Using a fork or slotted spoon, dip each cookie into the batter, coating it fully. Let the excess batter drip off, then place the cookies in the prepared basket in a single layer. Spritz each with cooking spray.

4. To prep the apple fries: Brush a crisper plate with the oil and install it in the Zone 2 basket.

5. In a large bowl, combine the flour, granulated sugar, baking powder, baking soda, and salt. Mix in the egg, almond milk, and vanilla to form a thick batter.

6. Core the apples and cut them into ½-inch-thick French fry shapes. Dust lightly with the cornstarch and apple pie spice.

7. Using a fork or slotted spoon, dip each apple into the batter, coating it fully. Let the excess batter drip off, then place the apples in the prepared basket in a single layer. Spritz with cooking spray.

8. To cook the "fried" Oreos and apple fries: Insert both baskets in the unit.

9. Select Zone 1, select AIR FRY, set the temperature to 400ºF, and set the timer to 8 minutes.

10. Select Zone 2, select AIR FRY, set the temperature to 400ºF, and set the timer to 10 minutes. Select SMART FINISH.™

11. Press START/PAUSE to begin cooking.

12. When cooking is complete, the batter will be golden brown and crisp. If desired, dust the cookies and apples with the powdered sugar before serving.

Mocha Pudding Cake // Vanilla Pudding Cake

SERVES 8

Pudding cakes were popular for a period of time when I was a kid, but I had completely forgotten about them until recently. I'm so glad I rediscovered them because they're so fun! The batter separates as it cooks, creating a cake on top and a rich pudding on the bottom. The pudding adds sweetness and moisture, so there's no need for frosting. This cake is delicious on its own, but for a real treat, top it off with a big scoop of ice cream or a dollop of whipped cream.

DAIRY-FREE, NUT-FREE, VEGAN

Prep time: 20 minutes, plus 10 minutes to cool
Cook time: 25 minutes

FOR THE MOCHA PUDDING CAKE

- 1 cup all-purpose flour
- ⅔ cup granulated sugar
- 1 cup packed light brown sugar, divided
- 5 tablespoons unsweetened cocoa powder, divided
- 2 teaspoons baking powder
- ¼ teaspoon kosher salt
- ½ cup unsweetened almond milk
- 2 teaspoons vanilla extract
- 2 tablespoons vegetable oil
- 1 cup freshly brewed coffee

FOR THE VANILLA PUDDING CAKE

- 1 cup all-purpose flour
- ⅔ cup granulated sugar, plus ½ cup
- 2 teaspoons baking powder
- ¼ teaspoon kosher salt
- ½ cup unsweetened almond milk
- 2½ teaspoons vanilla extract, divided
- 2 tablespoons vegetable oil
- ¾ cup hot water
- 2 teaspoons cornstarch

1. **To prep the mocha pudding cake:** In a medium bowl, combine the flour, granulated sugar, ½ cup of brown sugar, 3 tablespoons of cocoa powder, the baking powder, and salt. Stir in the almond milk, vanilla, and oil to form a thick batter.

2. Spread the batter in the bottom of the Zone 1 basket. Sprinkle the remaining ½ cup brown sugar and 2 tablespoons of cocoa powder in an even layer over the batter. Gently pour the hot coffee over the batter (do not mix).

3. To prep the vanilla pudding cake: In a medium bowl, combine the flour, ⅔ cup of granulated sugar, the baking powder, and salt. Stir in the almond milk, 2 teaspoons of vanilla, and the oil to form a thick batter.

4. Spread the batter in the bottom of the Zone 2 basket.

5. In a small bowl, whisk together the hot water, cornstarch, and remaining ½ cup of sugar and ½ teaspoon of vanilla. Gently pour over the batter (do not mix).

6. To cook both pudding cakes: Insert both baskets in the unit.

7. Select Zone 1, select BAKE, set the temperature to 330ºF, and set the timer to 25 minutes. Select MATCH COOK™ to match Zone 2 settings to Zone 1.

8. Press START/PAUSE to begin cooking.

9. When cooking is complete, the tops of the cakes should be dry and set.

10. Let the cakes rest for 10 minutes before serving. The pudding will thicken as it cools.

Per serving (mocha): *Calories: 531; Total fat: 8g; Saturated fat: 1g; Carbohydrates: 115g; Fiber: 3.5g; Protein: 5g; Sodium: 111mg*

Per serving (vanilla): *Calories: 409; Total fat: 7.5g; Saturated fat: 1g; Carbohydrates: 84g; Fiber: 1g; Protein: 3g; Sodium: 95mg*

Variation: For the mocha pudding cake, the coffee enhances the chocolaty flavor, but you can swap hot water or warm milk if you prefer.

MEASUREMENT CONVERSIONS

VOLUME EQUIVALENTS (LIQUID)

U.S. Standard	U.S. Standard (ounces)	Metric (approximate)
2 tablespoons	1 fl. oz.	30 mL
¼ cup	2 fl. oz.	60 mL
½ cup	4 fl. oz.	120 mL
1 cup	8 fl. oz.	240 mL
1½ cups	12 fl. oz.	355 mL
2 cups or 1 pint	16 fl. oz.	475 mL
4 cups or 1 quart	32 fl. oz.	1 L
1 gallon	128 fl. oz.	4 L

OVEN TEMPERATURES

Fahrenheit (F)	Celsius (C) (approximate)
250°F	120°C
300°F	150°C
325°F	165°C
350°F	180°C
375°F	190°C
400°F	200°C
425°F	220°C
450°F	230°C

VOLUME EQUIVALENTS (DRY)

U.S. Standard	Metric (approximate)
⅛ teaspoon	0.5 mL
¼ teaspoon	1 mL
½ teaspoon	2 mL
¾ teaspoon	4 mL
1 teaspoon	5 mL
1 tablespoon	15 mL
¼ cup	59 mL
⅓ cup	79 mL
½ cup	118 mL
⅔ cup	156 mL
¾ cup	177 mL
1 cup	235 mL
2 cups or 1 pint	475 mL
3 cups	700 mL
4 cups or 1 quart	1 L

WEIGHT EQUIVALENTS

U.S. Standard	Metric (approximate)
½ ounce	15 g
1 ounce	30 g
2 ounces	60 g
4 ounces	115 g
8 ounces	225 g
12 ounces	340 g
16 ounces or 1 pound	455 g

AIR FRY COOKING CHART

NOTE: Don't see the food you're looking for in the charts below? Find a similar food, and decrease cook time by 25%. For frozen foods, decrease the cook time on the packaging by 25%. For best results, check on food often, increasing cook time if necessary.

INGREDIENT	AMOUNT PER ZONE	PREPARATION	TOSS IN OIL
VEGETABLES			
Asparagus	1 bunch	Whole, stems trimmed	2 tsp
Beets	6-7 small	Whole	None
Bell peppers (for roasting)	3 small peppers	Whole	None
Broccoli	1 head	Cut in 1-inch florets	1 Tbsp
Brussels sprouts	1 lb	Cut in half, stem removed	1 Tbsp
Butternut squash	1 ½ lbs	Cut in ½-inch pieces	1 Tbsp
Carrots	1 lb	Peeled, cut in ½-inch pieces	1 Tbsp
Cauliflower	1 head	Cut in 1-inch florets	2 Tbsp
Corn on the cob	2 ears, cut in half	Husks removed	1 Tbsp
Green beans	1 bag (12 oz)	Trimmed	1 Tbsp
Kale (for chips)	5 cups, packed	Torn in pieces, stems removed	None
Mushrooms	8 oz	Rinsed, cut in quarters	1 Tbsp
Potatoes, russet	1 ½ lbs	Cut in 1-inch wedges	1 Tbsp
	1 lb	Hand-cut fries*, thin	½-3 Tbsp, canola
	1 lb	Hand-cut fries*, thick	½-3 Tbsp, canola
	3 whole (6-8 oz)	Pierced with fork 3 times	None
Potatoes, sweet	1 ½ lbs	Cut in 1-inch chunks	1 Tbsp
	3 whole (6-8 oz)	Pierced with fork 3 times	None
Zucchini	1 lb	Cut in quarters lengthwise, then cut in 1-inch pieces	1 Tbsp
POULTRY			
Chicken breasts	2 breasts (¾-1 ½ lbs each)	Bone in	Brushed with oil
	4 breasts (½-¾ lb each)	Boneless	Brushed with oil
Chicken thighs	2 thighs (6-10 oz each)	Bone in	Brushed with oil
	4 thighs (4-8 oz each)	Boneless	Brushed with oil
Chicken wings	2 lbs	Drumettes & flats	1 Tbsp
FISH & SEAFOOD			
Crab cakes	2 cakes (6-8 oz each)	None	Brushed with oil
Lobster tails	4 tails (3-4 oz each)	Whole	None
Salmon fillets	3 fillets (4 oz each)	None	Brushed with oil
Shrimp	1 lb	Whole, peeled, tails on	1 Tbsp

*After cutting potatoes, allow raw fries to soak in cold water for at least 30 minutes to remove unnecessary starch. Pat fries dry. The drier the fries, the better the results.

TEMP	SINGLE ZONE when cooking in one zone— not using the other zone.	DUALZONE when cooking in both zones— same or different foods.
390°F	8–12 mins	20–25 mins
390°F	30–35 mins	35–40 mins
390°F	10–15 mins	15–20 mins
390°F	8–10 mins	15–17 mins
400°F	15–20 mins	20–25 mins
390°F	20–25 mins	35–40 mins
390°F	13–16 mins	25–30 mins
390°F	17–20 mins	20–25 mins
390°F	12–15 mins	18–20 mins
390°F	8–10 mins	10–15 mins
300°F	7–9 mins	15–20 mins
390°F	7–9 mins	13–15 mins
400°F	20–22 mins	35–38 mins
400°F	20–24 mins	30–35 mins
400°F	19–24 mins	35–40 mins
400°F	30–35 mins	37–40 mins
400°F	15–20 mins	30–35 mins
400°F	36–42 mins	40–45 mins
390°F	15–18 mins	25–28 mins
390°F	25–30 mins	30–35 mins
390°F	22–24 mins	25–28 mins
390°F	22–28 mins	26–29 mins
390°F	18–22 mins	25–28 mins
390°F	18–22 mins	43–47 mins
390°F	5–10 mins	10–13 mins
390°F	5–8 mins	15–18 mins
400°F	7–12 mins	13–17 mins
390°F	7–10 mins	10–13 mins

AIR FRY COOKING CHART

NOTE: Don't see the food you're looking for in the charts below? Find a similar food, and decrease cook time by 25%. For frozen foods, decrease the cook time on the packaging by 25%. For best results, check on food often, increasing cook time if necessary.

INGREDIENT	AMOUNT PER ZONE	PREPARATION	TOSS IN OIL
BEEF			
Burgers	2 quarter-pound patties, 80% lean	½ inch thick	Brushed with oil
Steaks	2 steaks (8 oz each)	Whole	Brushed with oil
PORK			
Bacon	3 strips, cut in half	None	None
Pork chops	2 thick-cut, bone-in chops (10–12 oz each)	Bone in	Brushed with oil
	2 boneless chops (8 oz each)	Boneless	Brushed with oil
Pork tenderloins	1 lb	None	Brushed with oil
Sausages	5 sausages	None	None
FROZEN FOODS			
Chicken cutlets	3 cutlets	None	None
Chicken nuggets	1 box (12 oz)	None	None
Fish fillets	1 box (6 fillets)	None	None
Fish sticks	18 fish sticks (11 oz)	None	None
French fries	1 lb	None	None
French fries	2 lbs	None	None
Mozzarella sticks	1 box (11 oz)	None	None
Onion Rings	10 oz	None	None
Pizza rolls	1 bag (20 oz, 40 count)	None	None
Popcorn shrimp	1 box (14–16 oz)	None	None
Pot stickers	2 bags (10.5 oz)	None	1 Tbsp
Sweet potato fries	1 lb	None	None
Tater tots	1 lb	None	None

| | SINGLE ZONE | DUALZONE |
TEMP	when cooking in one zone—not using the other zone.	when cooking in both zones—same or different foods.
390°F	8-10 mins	10-13 mins
390°F	10-20 mins	14-18 mins
350°F	8-10 mins	9-12 mins
390°F	15-17 mins	23-27 mins
390°F	14-17 mins	17-20 mins
375°F	15-20 mins	25-30 mins
390°F	7-10 mins	17-22 mins
400°F	18-21 mins	20-25 mins
390°F	10-13 mins	18-21 mins
390°F	14-16 mins	17-22 mins
390°F	10-13 mins	16-19 mins
400°F	18-22 mins	28-32 mins
400°F	32-36 mins	50-55 mins
375°F	8-10 mins	10-12 mins
375°F	13-16 mins	18-22 mins
390°F	12-15 mins	15-18 mins
390°F	9-11 mins	14-18 mins
390°F	12-14 mins	16-18 mins
390°F	20-22 mins	30-32 mins
375°F	18-22 mins	25-27 mins

DEHYDRATE COOKING CHART

INGREDIENTS	PREPARATION
FRUITS & VEGETABLES	
Apples	Cored, cut in ⅛-inch slices, rinsed in lemon water, patted dry
Asparagus	Cut in 1-inch pieces, blanched
Bananas	Peeled, cut in ⅜-inch slices
Beets	Peeled, cut in ⅛-inch slices
Eggplant	Peeled, cut in ¼-inch slices, blanched
Fresh herbs	Rinsed, patted dry, stems removed
Ginger root	Cut in ⅜-inch slices
Mangoes	Peeled, cut in ⅜-inch slices, pit removed
Mushrooms	Cleaned with soft brush (do not wash)
Pineapple	Peeled, cored, cut in ⅜–½-inch slices
Strawberries	Cut in half or in ½-inch slices
Tomatoes	Cut in ⅜-inch slices or grated; steam if planning to rehydrate
MEAT, POULTRY, FISH	
Beef jerky	Cut in ¼-inch slices, marinated overnight
Chicken jerky	Cut in ¼-inch slices, marinated overnight
Salmon jerky	Cut in ¼-inch slices, marinated overnight
Turkey jerky	Cut in ¼-inch slices, marinated overnight

TEMP	SINGLE ZONE when cooking in one zone— not using the other zone.  DUALZONE when cooking in both zones— same or different foods.
	TIMES ARE THE SAME FOR BOTH ZONES
135°F	7-8 hours
135°F	6-8 hours
135°F	8-10 hours
135°F	6-8 hours
135°F	6-8 hours
135°F	4 hours
135°F	6 hours
135°F	6-8 hours
135°F	6-8 hours
135°F	6-8 hours
135°F	6-8 hours
135°F	6-8 hours
150°F	5-7 hours
150°F	5-7 hours
150°F	3-5 hours
150°F	5-7 hours

Using DualZone™ Technology: SMART FINISH™

SMART FINISH eliminates the need for back-to-back cooking. Now you can cook two different foods with two different cook times, and watch as they finish at the same time. Simply program each zone, and let the **SMART FINISH** feature do the rest.

CHOOSE ANY TWO	ADD ONE RECIPE PER ZONE
RECIPE	**AMOUNT**
Crab Cakes	2 crab cakes
Balsamic Roasted Tomatoes	2 pints cherry tomatoes
Maple Sage Pork Chops	2–3 boneless pork chops (4 oz each)
Cajun Russet Potatoes	4 medium potatoes, diced
Classic Meatloaf	1 lb meatloaf mix (beef, pork, veal)
Green Beans with Almonds	1 lb green beans, ends trimmed
Miso Glazed Salmon	3 salmon fillets (6 oz each)
Honey Hazelnut Brussels Sprouts	1 lb Brussels sprouts, cut in half
Buffalo Chicken Thighs	4 boneless skin-on chicken thighs (4–5 oz each)
Plant Based "Meat" Burger	1 lb plant-based ground "meat" (4 [4-oz] patties)
Mediterranean Cauliflower	1 head cauliflower, cut in 1/2-inch florets
French Fries	1 lb French fries

NOTE: For your own best results, start checking food for doneness 2 minutes before cook time is complete. Stop cooking at any time if the desired level of crispiness has been achieved, but make sure any raw proteins have reached a food-safe temperature.

MIX OR COMBINE THESE INGREDIENTS	FUNCTION	SET BOTH ZONES AND USE SMART FINISH TEMP/TIME
Brush with melted butter	Air Fry	390°F | 15 minutes
½ cup balsamic vinegar 1 Tbsp canola oil	Roast	390°F | 15 minutes
1 Tbsp canola oil 1 Tbsp maple syrup	Roast	390°F | 17–20 minutes
2 Tbsp canola oil 2 Tbsp Cajun seasoning	Air Fry	400°F | 30 minutes
¼ cup ketchup, ¼ cup yellow mustard, 1 egg, ½ cup panko breadcrumbs, ¼ cup Parmesan cheese	Air Fry	330°F | 35 minutes
2 Tbsp canola oil ½ cup sliced almonds	Air Fry	390°F | 15 minutes
2 Tbsp miso paste, 1 teaspoon canola oil Rub onto salmon	Air Fry	390°F | 15 minutes
2 Tbsp canola oil, ¼ cup honey, ½ cup chopped hazelnuts	Air Fry	390°F | 23 minutes
1 cup buffalo sauce, toss with chicken	Air Fry	400°F | 27 minutes
1 Tbsp minced garlic, 1 Tbsp minced onion	Air Fry	375°F | 20 minutes
½ cup tahini, 2 Tbsp canola oil	Air Fry	390°F | 35 minutes
Season as desired	Air Fry	400°F | 30 minutes

MIX AND MATCH RECIPE COOKING CHART

One of the fun things about this cookbook is that you can mix and match the recipes to match your mood, the occasion, or how much time you have. The book has 80 pairings, but that translates to a full 160 individual recipes! Below, you'll find a quick reference guide to them all. Keep in mind that the recipes in this book were all developed to make use of both baskets of the Ninja® Foodi® 2-Basket Air Fryer. If using just one basket, the cook time will be shorter, so be sure to check for doneness periodically to avoid overcooking. All of the recipes in the book were written so that you can easily follow the directions for just one of the two components. That way you can choose one of the proteins listed here and match it with a completely new side component. Use the information in the Time column below to help you in setting any Smart Finish™ or Match Cook™ functions.

PAGE	RECIPE	FUNCTION	TEMPERATURE	TIME
SEAFOOD				
155	"Fried" Fish	Air Fry	400ºF	13 minutes
148	Parmesan-Crusted Fish Sticks	Air Fry	390ºF	18 minutes
150	Pecan-Crusted Catfish Nuggets	Air Fry	390ºF	17 minutes
146	Blackened Mahimahi	Air Fry	380ºF	14 minutes
144	Broiled Teriyaki Salmon	Air Broil	450ºF	8 minutes
153	Tilapia with Mojo	Air Fry	390ºF	10 minutes
59	Bacon-Wrapped Scallops	Air Fry	400ºF	12 minutes
160	Bang Bang Shrimp	Air Fry	390ºF	13 minutes
162	Garlic Shrimp	Air Fry	390ºF	13 minutes
157	Shrimp Po'Boys	Air Fry	390ºF	13 minutes
164	Broiled Crab Cakes	Air Broil	400ºF	15 minutes
62	Crab Rangoon Dip	Bake	330ºF	15 minutes
VEGETABLES				
112	Roasted Asparagus and Mushroom Medley	Roast	400ºF	25 minutes
160	Roasted Bok Choy	Bake	370ºF	8 minutes
108	Garlicky Roasted Broccoli	Roast	390ºF	15 minutes
85	Roasted Lemon-Parmesan Broccoli	Roast	390ºF	15 minutes
168	Cacio e Pepe Brussels Sprouts	Roast	400ºF	25 minutes
110	Sweet Chili Brussels Sprouts	Air Fry	400ºF	20 minutes
170	Roasted Cabbage	Roast	330ºF	20 minutes
146	Honey-Roasted Carrots	Roast	400ºF	30 minutes
103	Turkey Meatloaf with Veggie Medley	Air Fry	390ºF	20 minutes
89	Cauliflower "Wings"	Air Fry	390ºF	25 minutes
78	Pineapple Cauliflower Rice	Air Broil	450ºF	12 minutes
180	Corn Fritters	Air Fry	375ºF	15 minutes
76	Street Corn	Air Broil	450ºF	12 minutes
144	Eggplant in Stir-Fry Sauce	Air Fry	390ºF	25 minutes

PAGE	RECIPE	FUNCTION	TEMPERATURE	TIME
175	Mediterranean Vegetable Salad	Roast	375°F	15 minutes
96	Roasted Green Bean Casserole	Roast	350°F	40 minutes
135	Roasted Green Beans and Shallots	Roast	400°F	20 minutes
87	Broiled Utica Greens	Air Broil	450°F	10 minutes
74	Crispy Kale Chips	Air Fry	300°F	15 minutes
150	"Fried" Okra	Air Fry	400°F	12 minutes
189	"Fried" Onion Rings	Air Fry	375°F	10 minutes
48	Charred Lemon Shishito Peppers	Air Fry	390°F	10 minutes
48	Miso-Glazed Shishito Peppers	Air Fry	390°F	10 minutes
91	"Fried" Pickles	Air Fry	400°F	15 minutes
93	Warm Baked Potato Salad	Bake	400°F	40 minutes
114	Barbecue Potato Chips	Air Fry	390°F	15 minutes
32	Breakfast Potatoes	Air Fry	400°F	35 minutes
133	Brown Sugar–Pecan Sweet Potatoes	Bake	400°F	45 minutes
119	Hasselback Potatoes	Bake	375°F	30 minutes
126	Lemon-Feta Baby Potatoes	Air Fry	400°F	40 minutes
137	Peppers, Potatoes, and Onions	Roast	375°F	20 minutes
172	Potato and Parsnip Latkes	Air Fry	375°F	15 minutes
131	Scalloped Potatoes and Cauliflower	Bake	350°F	45 minutes
155	Seasoned Potato Wedges	Air Fry	400°F	30 minutes
157	Sweet Potato Fries	Air Fry	400°F	30 minutes
72	Buttery Roasted Radishes	Roast	400°F	15 minutes
80	Roasted Snap Peas and Scallions	Roast	375°F	12 minutes
175	Spanakopita Rolls	Air Fry	375°F	10 minutes
123	Spinach-Artichoke Stuffed Mushrooms	Bake	370°F	15 minutes
139	Baked Brown Sugar Acorn Squash	Bake	400°F	20 minutes
178	Roasted Butternut Squash	Roast	400°F	40 minutes
98	Roasted Vegetable Salad	Roast	400°F	20 minutes

PAGE	RECIPE	FUNCTION	TEMPERATURE	TIME
54	Roasted Tomato Bruschetta	Air Broil	450ºF	12 minutes
83	Broiled Zucchini and Cherry Tomatoes	Air Broil	450ºF	10 minutes
187	Crispy Zucchini Noodles	Air Fry	400ºF	12 minutes
184	Zucchini Chips	Air Fry	400ºF	20 minutes
BEEF, PORK, AND LAMB				
112	Balsamic Steak Tips	Air Fry	400ºF	12 minutes
116	Beef and Bean Taquitos	Air Fry	390ºF	15 minutes
52	Beef Jerky	Dehydrate	150ºF	8 hours
114	Cheeseburgers	Air Fry	390ºF	12 minutes
108	Italian-Style Meatballs	Air Fry	400ºF	12 minutes
110	Mongolian Beef	Air Fry	390ºF	15 minutes
121	Roast Beef	Air Fry	375ºF	40 to 60 minutes
119	Strip Steaks	Air Fry	375ºF	20 minutes
135	Barbecue Ribs	Air Fry	375ºF	40 minutes
28	Coffee-Glazed Canadian Bacon	Air Fry	400ºF	5 minutes
131	Garlic-Rosemary Pork Loin	Air Fry	390ºF	50 minutes
137	Italian Sausages	Air Fry	390ºF	22 minutes
30	Maple Sausage Patties	Air Fry	375ºF	12 minutes
123	Pigs in a Blanket	Air Fry	370ºF	8 minutes
129	Pork Katsu	Air Fry	390ºF	15 minutes
133	Pork Tenderloin	Air Fry	390ºF	25 minutes
34	Sausage Hash	Air Fry	400ºF	30 minutes
126	Roast Souvlaki-Style Pork	Roast	390ºF	20 minutes
39	Sweet and Spicy Twisted Bacon	Air Fry	400ºF	12 minutes
139	Curry-Crusted Lamb Chops	Air Fry	400ºF	15 minutes
POULTRY				
74	Barbecue Chicken Drumsticks	Bake	390ºF	20 minutes
56	Buffalo Wings	Air Fry	390ºF	40 minutes

PAGE	RECIPE	FUNCTION	TEMPERATURE	TIME
76	Chicken Fajitas	Air Fry	390°F	20 minutes
85	Chicken Parmesan	Air Fry	390°F	18 minutes
87	Coconut Chicken Tenders	Air Fry	390°F	25 minutes
93	"Fried" Chicken	Air Fry	390°F	30 minutes
83	Goat Cheese–Stuffed Chicken Breast	Air Fry	390°F	25 minutes
56	Honey-Garlic Wings	Air Fry	390°F	40 minutes
72	Lemon-Pepper Chicken Thighs	Air Fry	390°F	28 minutes
80	Orange Chicken	Air Fry	400°F	30 minutes
89	Roasted Garlic Chicken Pizza	Roast	375°F	25 minutes
91	Spicy Chicken Sandwiches	Air Fry	390°F	18 minutes
78	Sweet-and-Sour Chicken	Air Fry	400°F	30 minutes
101	Maple-Mustard Glazed Turkey Tenderloin	Air Fry	390°F	35 minutes
98	Ranch Turkey Tenders	Air Fry	375°F	20 minutes
96	Air-Fried Turkey Breast	Air Fry	360°F	50 minutes
103	Turkey Meatloaf	Roast	350°F	30 minutes
EGGS				
32	Baked Mushroom and Mozzarella Frittata	Bake	350°F	30 minutes
28	Spinach and Red Pepper Egg Cups	Bake	325°F	13 minutes
FRUITS				
50	Dried Apple Chips	Dehydrate	135°F	8 hours
172	Baked Apples	Bake	330°F	20 minutes
50	Dried Banana Chips	Dehydrate	135°F	10 hours
196	Banana Spring Rolls	Air Fry	390°F	10 minutes
59	Bacon-Wrapped Dates	Air Fry	360°F	10 minutes
24	Roasted Stone Fruit Compote	Roast	350°F	20 minutes
52	Pineapple Jerky	Dehydrate	135°F	12 hours
206	Roasted Strawberries	Roast	330°F	20 minutes

PAGE	RECIPE	FUNCTION	TEMPERATURE	TIME
	BREADS AND GRAINS			
101	Apple and Sage Stuffing	Bake	340ºF	20 minutes
41	Cinnamon-Raisin Bagels	Air Fry	325ºF	14 minutes
41	Everything Bagels	Air Fry	325ºF	14 minutes
24	Buttermilk Biscuits	Air Fry	400ºF	10 minutes
54	Toasty Garlic Bread	Air Fry	390ºF	10 minutes
164	Hush Puppies	Air Fry	400ºF	7 minutes
39	Pumpkin French Toast Casserole	Bake	330ºF	35 minutes
62	Crispy Wonton Strips	Air Fry	350ºF	6 minutes
64	Tortilla Chips	Air Fry	375ºF	5 minutes
121	Yorkshire Pudding	Bake	400ºF	20 minutes
36	Chocolate Peanut Butter Baked Oats	Bake	320ºF	15 minutes
36	Strawberry Baked Oats	Bake	320ºF	15 minutes
148	Baked Macaroni and Cheese	Bake	360ºF	25 minutes
68	"Fried" Ravioli	Air Fry	390ºF	20 minutes
162	Pasta Alfredo	Bake	360ºF	40 minutes
129	Seasoned Rice	Bake	350ºF	10 minutes
116	Mexican Rice	Bake	350ºF	10 minutes
	CAKE, PASTRY, AND SWEET SAUCES			
44	Glazed Apple Fritters	Air Fry	345ºF	10 minutes
194	Apple Crumble	Bake	350ºF	20 minutes
212	Apple Fries	Air Fry	400ºF	10 minutes
30	Blueberry Coffee Cake	Bake	350ºF	25 minutes
209	Blueberry Hand Pies	Air Fry	350ºF	15 minutes
198	Caramel Sauce	Bake	350ºF	10 minutes
26	Cherry Danishes	Air Fry	330ºF	15 minutes
198	Cinnamon-Sugar "Churros"	Air Fry	330ºF	10 minutes
200	Cinnamon-Sugar Tortillas	Air Fry	375ºF	5 minutes

PAGE	RECIPE	FUNCTION	TEMPERATURE	TIME
206	Fried Dough	Air Fry	400ºF	18 minutes
212	"Fried" Oreos	Air Fry	400ºF	8 minutes
196	Hot Fudge Dip	Bake	330ºF	8 minutes
204	Lemon Sugar Cookie Bars	Bake	330ºF	18 minutes
26	Lemon-Cream Cheese Danishes	Air Fry	330ºF	15 minutes
214	Mocha Pudding Cake	Bake	330ºF	25 minutes
204	Monster Sugar Cookie Bars	Bake	330ºF	18 minutes
194	Peach Crumble	Bake	350ºF	20 minutes
44	Glazed Peach Fritters	Air Fry	345ºF	12 minutes
202	Pistachio Baklava Bites	Bake	330ºF	10 minutes
209	Pumpkin Hand Pies	Air Fry	350ºF	15 minutes
200	S'mores Dip	Bake	330ºF	5 minutes
214	Vanilla Pudding Cake	Bake	330ºF	25 minutes
202	Walnut Baklava Bites	Bake	330ºF	10 minutes
VEGETARIAN MAINS				
168	Air-Fried Tofu Cutlets	Air Fry	400ºF	20 minutes
178	Balsamic-Glazed Tofu	Air Fry	400ºF	10 minutes
187	Buffalo Seitan	Bake	360ºF	12 minutes
184	Caprese Panini	Air Fry	375ºF	20 minutes
170	Jerk Tofu	Air Fry	390ºF	15 minutes
180	Satay-Style Tempeh	Air Broil	400ºF	8 minutes
189	Veggie Burgers	Air Fry	390ºF	25 minutes
MISCELLANEOUS				
64	Jalapeño Popper Dip	Bake	350ºF	15 minutes
66	Crispy Chickpeas	Air Fry	375ºF	20 minutes
182	Croutons	Bake	390ºF	10 minutes
182	Crispy Fried Goat Cheese	Air Fry	400ºF	6 minutes
68	Zesty Marinara	Bake	350ºF	15 minutes
153	Crispy Plantains	Air Fry	390ºF	30 minutes

INDEX

ABOUT THE AUTHOR

 **Lauren Keating** is the author behind the blog Healthy Delicious, where she has been sharing easy weeknight recipes made with fresh, nutritious ingredients for over a decade. Lauren studied plant-based professional cooking through Rouxbe cooking school and uses those skills to incorporate fruits, vegetables, and whole grains into her recipes in unique ways. She lives in Upstate New York with her husband, Shawn, and their two dogs. Lauren lives by the motto: If it isn't delicious, it isn't worth eating. This is her fifth cookbook.

Printed in the USA
CPSIA information can be obtained
at www.ICGtesting.com
CBHW070839170224
4317CB00012B/7